Waxing Femininity

Adult Female Development from the Perspective of C. G. Jung's Psychology

Pia Skogemann is a Jungian analyst with an academic background in Archaeology and Comparative Religion (M.A.). In private practice since 1978, she co-founded the C.G. Jung Institute in Copenhagen in 1980, where her deep commitment to the field has seen her actively involved as a teacher, supervisor, and director of training for over four decades. Known for her thoughtful contributions to Jungian psychology, Skogemann became an individual member of the International Association for Analytical Psychology (IAAP) in 1986 and later served on its executive committee from 2001 to 2007. Her extensive bibliography, which includes numerous books and articles, reflects her diverse interests and expertise, though much of her published work is in Danish. A complete list of her writings can be found at www.piaskogemann.dk.

Pia Skogemann

WAXING FEMININITY

Adult Female Development from the
Perspective of C. G. Jung's Psychology

JUNGIANEUM
RE - COVERED CLASSICS
IN ANALYTICAL PSYCHOLOGY
SERIES EDITOR STEFANO CARPANI

Waxing Femininity: Adult Female Development from the Perspective of C.G. Jung's Psychology

First Edition

Copyright © 1984-2024 by Pia Skogemann

First published in 1984 by Kvindelighed i vækst. Lindhardt og Ringhof, Kbh. 1984. Later published in 1988 by Lindhardt og Ringhof, Kbh. Republished in 2023 by Saxo.com.

Cover and interior designed by Niko Crnčević

Independently published by Pia Skogemann, with the collaborative expertise of JUNGIANEUM.

ISBN 9798341126589

Table of Contents

Editor's Introduction   VII

Foreword to the Current Edition   XI

Introduction to the Current Edition   I

Chapter 1:
THE JOURNEY TO CRETE   5

Chapter 2:
THE MAN IN THE WOMAN: ANIMUS   19

Chapter 3:
ANIMUS DEVELOPMENT IN THE INDIVIDUATION PROCESS   59

Chapter 4:
THE WOMAN AND THE FEMININE   77

Chapter 5:
FEMALE INDIVIDUATION   103

Bibliography   161

Editor's Introduction

Pia Skogemann's *Waxing Femininity*, originally published in Danish in 1984 and now available for the first time in English, continues the mission of this series to highlight the theme of the feminine and femininity in contemporary society[1].

In *Waxing Femininity*, as aptly noted in the foreword by IAAP President Misser Berg, "Skogemann describes the feminine development from the little girl to the mature woman—how the girl meets and relates to the mother, the father, and the opposite sex, and how she gradually develops her own personal identity."

We chose to republish Skogemann's work because we believe it remains a foundational piece in contemporary post-Jungian thought that deserves renewed attention. This is further emphasized by the rich inclusion of dreams and case studies that seek to support women in discovering their own identities.

I would like to express my deepest thanks to Misser Berg for her insightful foreword to this edition, and to Niko Crnčević for his invaluable contribution in helping bring this important work back into print.

The aim of this series, *Re-Covered Classics in Analytical Psychology*, which I started in 2022, is to (re)publish masterpieces in analytical psychology that, for different reasons, are out of the market and that find difficulty in getting (re)published. *Re-Covered Classics in Analytical Psychology* is an initiative for (re)publishing high standard and academic work in the field of analytical psychology

---

[1] This focus began with the republication of Polly Young-Eisendrath's *Women and Desire: Beyond Wanting to Be Wanted* (2023).

(with a strong interdisciplinary flavor focusing on psychoanalysis at large). This initiative is driven by necessity, as the publishing market had changed in recent years due to the digitalization on the publishing industry, the fact that online shops increased in market dominance and aggressively lowered the profitability of traditional publishing houses. As a result, there are very few companies continuing to survive on the old model of large print runs, warehousing books, and full upfront "good faith" investment upon acceptance of a manuscript for publication.

Also, historical Jungian publishers are rapidly shutting down or are no longer accepting titles. This situation has left a gaping hole whereby up-and-coming and forward-thinking scholars of the Jungian, analytical field lack access to a wider audience and the means to contribute to the greater intellectual and psychosocial/mental health readership communities.

Therefore, I developed this series to preserve the work of our ancestors and to make them available again to the public. I doubt this series will be a profitable experience. For sure it will be a romantic one, whose aim is to preserve culture!

The publication of this book is independent and facilitated by *Jungianeum: Contemporary Initiatives for Analytical Psychology and Neo-Jungian Studies.* Under this umbrella, since 2022, I am developing a series of initiatives called: *JUNGIANEUM/Books Series: Re-Covered Classics in Analytical Psychology and Neo-Jungian Studies; JUNGIANEUM/Talks: Psychosocial Wednesday; JUNGIANEUM/Yearbook for Contemporary neo-Jungian Studies; JUNGIANEUM/Masterclasses* (in collaboration with Pacifica Graduate Institute, USA); *JUNGIANEUM/Cultivating the Souls in the Supersociety* (interview series on doppiozero.it).

Collection

- Verena Kast, *Father-Daughter, Mother-Son* (2022)
- Polly Young-Eisendrath, Women and Desire: *Beyond Wanting to Be Wanted* (2023)
- Mary Watkins, *Opening to the Imaginal: Waking Dreams and Invisible Guests* (2024)
- Pia Skogemann, Waxing Femininity: *Adult Female Development from the Perspective of C. G. Jung's Psychology* (2024)
- Mario Jacoby, Verena Kast, Ingrid Riedel, *Witches, Ogres, and the Devil's Daughter: Encounters With Evil in Fairy Tales* (Forthcoming, 2025)
- Thomas Singer & Stuart Copans, *Who's the Patient Here?: Portraits of the Young Psychotherapist* (Forthcoming, 2025)
- John Beebe, Psychiatric Treatment: *Crisis, Clinic, Consultation* (Forthcoming, 2025)

Stefano Carpani, Berlin (Germany)

Foreword to the Current Edition

I am delighted to write the preface to Pia Skogemann's book *Waxing Femininity* which has been a continuous bestseller during the last four decades in Denmark. Despite previous translations into a number of foreign languages, this is the first, and in my mind most welcome, English translation.

The book was first published in 1984 – a fertile period in Jungian theory where several female post-Jungians used existing Jungian theories as a starting point for their own theoretical developments. Pia Skogemann was one of the first of those.

In those years, the Jungian theory as a whole experienced a major resurgence. At Danish universities, e.g., students wrote about Animus and Anima in their literary studies, and many of the Jungian concepts, such as the shadow, archetypes, complexes, etc., also found their way into media, etc. (This development has continued ever since, and many of the words have become common language. Now few people associate those words with Jung).

At the same time, however, parts of the Jungian theory had become inadequate for women of that time. They had experienced and taken part in the second-wave feminism in the 1960s and 70s that focused on critiquing patriarchal, or male-dominated, institutions and cultural practices throughout society, de facto inequalities, and official legal inequalities; although Jung was much more aware of the feminine area than his predecessors, his descriptions clearly showed that he was a man of his time. And none of his early theoretical followers, e.g., Marie Louise von Franz,

Emma Jung, Toni Wolf, and Erich Neumann, really took a critical look at this basic view of the feminine. Instead, they expanded and interpreted Jung's theories and gave us many invaluable contributions.

It was typical for the new creative generation of female Jungians in the 1980s, in addition to Pia Skogemann, Silvia Brinton Perera, Marion Woodman, Linda Schierce Leonard, and others, that they also used much of the existing theory, both from Jung and his early followers, but they were much more critical and added their own, often personally experienced corrections and additions to the whole. It had become increasingly difficult, especially for active and clear-thinking women, to see themselves described as animus-possessed and to read the unflattering characteristics of their behavior. The description of the female was simply outdated. Finding our own female identity became very important for many of us who could not identify with the patriarchal norms that reduced us to perform qualities or roles that were not founded in our own experiences but in a traditional view of femininity shaped by the male-dominated culture.

On this background, Pia Skogemann's book fell on dry land. It quickly became a bestseller because it gave many of us women a direction away from our gender uncertainty and showed us new ways to develop, not by following the well-described phases of masculine individuation, but on the contrary, by searching for descriptions of female individuation. As Pia Skogemann writes, the problem is that the existing descriptions are almost always seen from the side of male psychology. But the woman's quest for her own identity seems to a certain degree to be different from the man's hero journey, and it was really attractive for many of us to explore this new area.

In *Waxing Femininity*, Pia Skogemann describes the feminine development from the little girl to the mature woman. How the girl meets and relates to the mother, the father, and the opposite sex, and how she gradually develops her own personal identity. As already mentioned, the texts in the book are building upon the already well-known Jungian concepts, but the interpretations of how these concepts express themselves are very different from the original descriptions. To illustrate her own theories, Pia Skogemann includes many dreams and case material as well as material from an interesting study of women authors' descriptions of their female protagonist's journey to find her own identity (p. 98)

When the book was first published, it was seen as provocative and challenging, and not everybody liked it. I remember how some women, at one of Pia Skogemann's lectures on the book, walked out of the room in anger. But for many of us, it was a gift that gave us a much better grounding in the world and a much better ability to speak with our own voices.

It has given me great pleasure to see the repetitive reprints over the years. The latest, as far as I can see, was in March 2023. It is also a pleasure to see how useful the book is and has been over the years for our candidates at the G.G. Jung Institute in Copenhagen. It is my hope that this English edition will reach a large audience - it would be well deserved!

Misser Berg
IAAP President
Copenhagen (Denmark)

Introduction to the Current Edition

It has been 40 years since the publication of this book in Denmark, and I am happy to see it revived in English. Over these decades, the therapy market has expanded significantly, and certain concepts have transcended beyond Jungian circles, particularly the idea of women in therapy expressing a desire to explore "their masculine sides." However, the real imperative lies in addressing the feminine. The challenge arises from the traditional understanding of both masculine and feminine qualities, providing little guidance for female development. In the latter part of my book, I endeavored to outline a female pattern for individuation distinct from the classical hero myth pattern and introduced the concept of the daughter archetype. As time progressed, I recognized the need to refine its theoretical underpinnings, leading to my current perspective:

I define the daughter archetype as a fundamental concept representing a woman as a subject in her own right, offering a framework for female agency that is otherwise absent in analytical psychology. The term is intentionally distinct from the mother archetype. While the notion addresses the female psyche, it refrains from defining the feminine per se. The daughter archetype's phenomenology manifests across all levels of psychic functioning, ranging from developmental level, everyday level, to archetypal level and goddess-like Self-representations:

Developmental Level: In the normal development of girls, the imagery of the daughter archetype unfolds in plays, dreams, and heroines embraced by young girls—from early pink princess fantasies and playing with Barbie dolls to characters like Pippi Longstocking. In adult analysis, daughter archetype images often mediate aspects of the Self, requiring conscious acknowledgment and integration into the female personality to facilitate individuation. They support differentiation from traditional gender roles and identification with anima projections from men, fostering the development of ego consciousness and autonomy. Differentiation between the Mother archetype and the Daughter archetype is crucial for women, akin to the differentiation of the anima from the mother archetype in men.

Everyday Level: This refers to socially recognized gender roles for young women, whose symbolic dimensions become visible only when critically examined and detached from absoluteness. On an individual level, these roles are often conflated with the persona or projections of the anima from men. Contemporary young women enjoy greater freedom in lifestyle choices, education, profession, and relationships with both women and men, a significant departure from the limited choices of earlier generations.

Archetypal Level: The daughter archetype is intricately woven into symbols throughout history, including mythology and fairy tales. Jung himself discussed one version of the archetypal daughter in his article 'The Psychological Aspects of the Kore,' associating the figure of Kore with the anima archetype when observed in both men and women. The passive, abducted Kore type corresponds to conservative gender roles or, in my view, a poorly developed ego, as seen in the Greek myth where the female agency is exclusively held by the mother goddess, Demeter. One striking example of a mighty Daughter Goddess is the Sumerian Inanna. Another is the Biblical Sophia, the Wisdom of God, e.g., depicted in Michelangelo's famous painting of the Creation of Adam as a beautiful young woman in God's arms, assisting in the Creation. My concept of the daughter archetype does not challenge our fundamental Jungian concepts but questions the use of binary-gendered properties in the theoretical couples: anima and animus, the feeling and thinking function in the psychological typology, Eros and Logos, and matriarchal and patriarchal consciousness.

I view anima and animus as fundamental clinical tools referring to unconscious phenomenology in dreams and projections, while the feeling and thinking function describes the workings of the conscious mind. Although a feeling-type woman may often associate with a thinking animus, the reverse may be true for a thinking-type woman. In dreams, I have observed the daughter archetype appearing in adult women's dreams and fantasies, similar to how other analysts describe the anima in women. I choose to retain the terms anima and animus, reserving anima for male fantasies about women and the feminine and animus for female fantasies about men and the masculine.

Jung defined Eros as psychic relatedness and Logos as objective interest, identifying anima with Eros and animus with Logos, thus collapsing the first three concepts into gender stereotypes. But it is not necessary to stick to that interpretation, and I still find the concepts very useful when adapted to the present.

Thank you to Stefano Carpani for the initiative and to JUNGIANEUM/Books for taking on the publishing. And thank you to all the women – and men – who read my book in the years gone by.

Pia Skogemann
Copenhagen (Denmark), September 2024

Chapter I

The Journey to Crete

Island of the Mother Goddess: Jung and the Archetypes

- "Have you had a dream recently?"
- "Yes, last night". I responded. And continued: "I dreamt that I won a fortune. I wanted to go to Crete, and I invited all sorts of people to join me on the flight. Finally, I saw that we were landing on a beach as the sun was setting".
- "Have you been to Crete?"
- "No."
- "It must be the mythical Crete, then."

This is a brief recollection of my first conversation with Said Eigil Nyborg, who would become my guide on the journey into the Jungian universe. During that meeting, which took place over a dozen years ago, I shared a dream that had deeply stirred me. At the time, I was captivated by the idea of becoming an analyst and equally enchanted by a few Jungian texts I had encountered. I had little more to offer than my fascination and a powerful instinct, embodied in that dream, which told me unmistakably that the time was NOW.

Much later, when I was about to begin my first analytical work under supervision, I had a special experience. I was finally really on my way to Crete. Somewhere over Greece, I began to have a sense of déjà vu and then remembered my old dream. I told my companion about it, describing how we would soon be landing with the beach and the sea on our left as the sun was setting. We exchanged knowing glances as, a few moments later, the plane touched down on the runway at Heraklion. To our left, the setting sun colored the Mediterranean purple-red.

The rest of the holiday was fine and not very mysterious. This is an example of how internal and external events can sometimes overlap. But I do not think my dream's message was exhausted with that.

In a way, the fortune I won in the dream is similar to the experience I had with C.G. Jung's psychology. A great wealth, a living experience. With this book, I wanted to invite "all sorts of people" on a trip to Crete. To the mythical Crete that I know more about now than I did ten years ago. My own inner journey there has brought me to the theme of this book: female psychology.

Island of the Mother Goddess

Mythical Crete is the island of the Great Mother Goddess. It was there before Greek patriarchal culture flourished. It was there that the great Greek god Zeus was born and nourished by bees. It was there that Theseus defeated the monster Minotaur with the help of the wise Ariadne but then shamefully abandoned her. She was left on an island where the god Dionysus took her as his bride, and her golden bridal wreath can still be seen in the sky as the constellation Ariadne's wreath. But that is almost all we have seen of Ariadne since then. The traces of female wisdom combined with Dionysian ecstasy must nowadays be unearthed by the unconscious. Here, they have rested throughout the patriarchal culture.

To describe female psychology, we have to turn the myth upside down in a way. From a female developmental point of view, Theseus is the woman's own masculine side, which she has to get to know anew. We need to look at how the patriarchal an xboximus plays out in the psyche of the woman and how she can prevent "him" from leaving her in the arms of a god who will forever stand as the one she loved in vain and who ended up becoming her enemy. We must also look at the meaning of marriage to Dionysus, the god of ecstasy and intoxication. How can female wisdom return from the celestial regions – or the collective unconscious – and approach the earthly sphere again? Women who have associated themselves with such gods in a Christian patriarchal culture have taken on the character of witches. If the culture does not accept the Dionysian, then it is not given any consciously formed expression and is instead demonized. We know this very well: woman as a temptress, the work of evil.

Nowadays, however, the conditions for the multifaceted expression of femininity have improved. This does not mean, however, that women today should simply put a positive spin on what used to be negative – and unreflectively identify with it. There would then be no real synthesis of the old contradictions between the matriarchal and the patriarchal, but merely a change of sign.

A real change in the feminine must come through the conscious integration of these ancient archetypal images into the psyche of men and women alike. This will involve psychological growth.

Jung and the Archetypes

In a very short time, I have managed to use a lot of technical terms: dream, analyst, mythical, archetypal, collective unconscious, animus, integration, and psychological growth. And behind all this is C.G. Jung.

Before I begin my actual theme, I will therefore give a brief presentation of Jung's theory and concepts. Jung, as most people will know, was Sigmund Freud's somewhat younger contemporary. They worked closely together for several years, so closely that Freud even wanted to make Jung his 'crown prince.' Yet their paths diverged, and their theories developed very differently. Jung sees the psyche as made up of roughly three layers. The consciousness, the personal unconscious, and the collective (transpersonal) unconscious.

In consciousness, the *ego* rules. It constitutes a 'complex,' a center of what we know consciously or can call up in consciousness without much difficulty. The *personal unconscious* contains all the matter that the conscious mind has repressed or forgotten completely. This material tends to accumulate in partially *autonomous* (independently acting) *complexes.* We are talking about father complexes, mother complexes, inferiority complexes, and many others. These are highly emotional areas in the life of the soul, which you will probably realize if you unknowingly bump into a complex in another person. The contents of the complexes contain material that is not immediately acceptable to consciousness. If, for example, one's father appears to one as an ideal, omniscient figure, there will be all sorts of traits in the father complex that also belong to the father but are less nice. Awareness of such a complex will, therefore, involve beginning to see the father as a real person, for better or worse.

Since every complex involves many different factors, each of which is active in its own way in the unconscious, we speak of a complex being *constellated* when a number of dream motifs can be traced back to a common denominator, which in this case would be the father complex. Similarly, we speak of an archetype being constellated. It is the whole that arises from the combination of different parts that form the constellation, just as the individual stars in the sky only form a constellation when they are combined to make up a constellation.

As soon as you begin to realize the personal unconscious, you will also encounter the *shadow*. It has all the traits that your personality also contains but has not realized. It is called a shadow because the ego represents the light of consciousness, which casts a shadow over what the ego does not know. But in itself, the shadow is not necessarily evil. It can also contain positive abilities and possibilities that were just not realized. The elements of the unconscious are usually experienced in projected form. *Projection* means seeing in others what really belongs to oneself and usually also seeing it in a distorted form, whether it is idealized or devalued. The shadow is projected onto people of the same sex as oneself.

On the borderline between the personal unconscious and the collective unconscious are the opposite-sex parts of us. The male part of the woman is called *animus,* and the female part of the man is *anima.* We are not talking about a man's animus or a woman's anima. These figures are projected onto persons of the opposite sex. (There are exceptions to these rules of thumb, but I won't go into them here).

Through awareness of the shadow and animus/anima, we can differentiate and integrate their content. To *differentiate* means to learn to discern differences and nuances where previously these were not perceived. To *integrate* something means to include a hitherto unknown or unaccepted factor as a conscious part of the personality. These two factors are part of all development and are not confined to working with the unconscious in the adult person.

There is an external, social part to animus/anima that coincides with gender roles. When a woman becomes a crane operator and a man becomes a nurse, she is functioning in a male gender role, and he is in a female one. However, this need not necessarily be an integration of the opposite-sexed parts but can often correspond to an *identification with* animus/anima. The decisive factor is not the gender role behavior but an individual psychological experience, which must necessarily have a basis in the primary gender identity. Gender roles are social factors, and their greater flexibility in modern society in no way solves the individual's psychological problems.

Jung saw it as an ideal that men and women differentiate and integrate their opposite-sex parts. He realized early on the necessity of women's emancipation. In 1927, he wrote[2]:

> *We can see that woman is in the process of breaking with the purely feminine sexual pattern of unconsciousness and passivity, and has made a concession to masculine psychology by establishing herself as a visible member of society. She no longer hides behind the mask of Mrs So-and-so with the obliging intention of having all her wishes fulfilled by the man or to make him pay for it if things do not go as she wishes.*

A few lines in, he makes a reservation that shows that Jung, for all his foresight, is still living in his time – and Switzerland in 1927 was a very conservative place:

> *Certainly, the courage and capacity for self-sacrifice of such women is admirable, and only a blind man could fail to see the good that has*

---

[2] Women in Europe

come out of all these efforts. But no one can get around the fact that by taking up a masculine profession, studying and working like a man, a woman is doing something not wholly in accord with, if not directly injurious to, her feminine nature. She is doing something that would scarcely be possible for a man to do unless he were Chinese. Could he, for instance, be a nursemaid or run a kindergarten?

Well, we all know that in today's Denmark, men can do that. They can also take care of babies. Most of Jung's work on the female in the man reflects the starting point that the man is far too much of a man and, therefore, only experiences the female in projected form. Similarly, the work on the masculine in the woman reflects a very traditional female role. Compared to this point of departure, we have a completely different psychological situation in the present time. Projections still play a major role, of course, but so does the identification with animus/anima. Probably, it would be appropriate to ask whether this dissolution of gender boundaries has really, as Jung says, caused psychological harm to men and women.

In a way, you must agree with Jung. Today, there are many people who are swamped by their opposite-sex parts; in the therapeutic work with them, one must actually begin by anchoring the primary gender identity. But the crucial point, from my point of view, is that the psychological solution to these problems lies in no way in a return – but rather in an expansion of consciousness large enough to accommodate a synthesis of male and female qualities in the individual. That is to say, an approximation to a dual-gender ideal that has been unthinkable in the past.

This means – since it is clear from Jung's writings – that on a psychological level, it was not at all unthinkable for him. Where he, in a way, sets some limits at the practical level. His visions turned inwards in his mind, not outwards, and one can hardly blame him for not being able to foresee the social changes of the last couple of decades. One could say that the collective unconscious has moved closer. What was relatively rare in Jung's time is now more commonplace. The widespread interest in recent years in the inner world and its mythical content seems to confirm this. Consequently, there is also greater interest in Jung's pioneering work today than in the first many years after his death in 1961. What once seemed cryptic and mysterious to the outside world and was therefore rejected is now presented in a much more accessible form, for example, by Stanislav Grof, who, from a different angle in many ways, confirms Jung's ideas.

The problem is that what becomes commonplace is also easily trivialized. You come to believe that you can get it all quite cheaply on a weekend course or two. Of course, you can't. Personal development is the most expensive thing you can buy in this world because it requires a lifetime of effort.

You invest everything you have in the hope of regaining your authentic Self. In many myths and fairy tales, the hero does indeed win the treasure but loses it again because he is momentarily inattentive. It is a lifelong task to be aware of the actual values of one's life.

What are we to understand by the *collective unconscious*? It is the part of the psyche that is common to all human beings. As individuals, we are different, but as human beings, we are very similar. Physically and psychologically, we have grown from a single root back at the dawn of time.

The basic human condition has always had much in common. The expressions of cultures and religions are richly varied, but they must all try to come to terms with some absolutes without which human beings are no longer human beings – or no longer *exist* at all.

Through the study of human history, we can learn about human behavior. Through the study of people's religious and spiritual lives, we can learn about the inner side of people. Today, we can directly observe the inner life through dreams, fantasies, and creative expressions.

Jung believed that human beings were not only biologically but also psychologically 'programmed' for human existence. The basic 'program' of the psyche is the *archetypes*. Jung inferred the existence of archetypes from the archetypal *images*. These are the ever-recurring typical motifs that appear in myths, fairy tales, fantasies, dreams, and delusions. Although the forms of these motifs are richly varied, they can nevertheless be linked to basic human conditions and situations. Their independent activity in the psyche is demonstrated, for example, by the fact that motives can emerge in a person's unconscious material, which can in no way be derived from personal experience or knowledge.

Jung saw archetypes as the psychological equivalents of instincts, the existence of which cannot be proved but only inferred from typical behavior. Now, it could very well be that if we could talk to the animals, we could learn that they also had inner experiences in connection with mating rituals or nest-building, just as we do, perhaps even of a kind that we might characterize as spiritual. But we cannot know anything about that for the time being. In any case, there seems to be a difference between humans and other animals in that humans are relatively less bound by instinctive impulses. A female ape cannot voluntarily refrain from having young, but a woman can if something else in her life seems to her sufficiently important. (I mean voluntarily, not neurotically conditioned.) The archetypes must be understood as a field linked, on the one hand, to instinctive activity and, on the other, to spiritual activity. One cannot reduce the one to the other, and thus, one cannot conceive of cultural creations as sublimated sexuality.

Jung labelled the archetypes as *psychoid*; that is, he believed that their true nature could not be made conscious because it is transcendent (transgressive) to the human psyche. On the one hand, the human psyche may reflect something that appears to be an objective, divine factor and is certainly perceived as such by many people. On the other hand, the psyche seems to be connected not only with man's own physical life but also with the inorganic basis of life itself, namely matter.

Jung did not end up in the classical, dualistic worldview, where the material, physical world faces a spiritual, transcendent world. He dared to hypothesize a unified world, a *Unus Mundus*, where everything is connected to everything else. This Unus Mundus idea appears, e.g., in the classical Chinese symbol, in which yin and yang are joined in the unity of the Tao, and in the Indian Mandala images. Jung discovered that similar symbols were spontaneously produced by his patients who had no knowledge of these foreign religions.

He also found a parapsychological equivalent to this, which he described as *synchronicity* or the meaningful coincidence of internal psychic events and external occurrences. Most others who have taken an interest in parapsychology attempt to explain it in terms of our usual scientific way of thinking, that of causation. For example, that telepathy takes place from a 'sender' to a 'receiver.' Jung believes that such things can happen because we are all part of the same unitary world and that communication takes place via the activities of the archetype in the unconscious. This explains, for example, why the subjective interest of subjects in parapsychological laboratories is so important. In these cases, as in other spontaneous cases, there must be an emotional preoccupation in order for the unconscious to manifest itself and the "message" to reach consciousness as an image or impression.

Experience with analytical psychology seems to show that such phenomena occur more frequently than might be supposed, probably not least because people are aware of the possibility. For example, a man meets by chance a girl he has been in love with at school and has not seen for 20 years. She tells him that she has recently been hospitalized with acute psychosis. What particularly impresses him is neither the meeting with his old love nor her problem, but the fact that he has just dreamt about her for the first time and has begun to realize that his previous development has, in fact, steered him dangerously close to psychosis. If he were not in the process of being analyzed, the encounter with the girl would hardly be seen as anything other than a coincidence.

The psychological parallel to Jung's metaphysical Unus Mundus concept is the archetype of the Self. It is the central archetype that is the center of the psyche as a whole, in a similar way as the ego is the center of consciousness. Since the Self is perceived as a transcendent factor, it is not easy to determine where the Self ends and the World Self, or Unus Mundus, begins. This is the metaphysical paradox expressed in the Upanishadic statement: Atman (the personal Self) equals Brahman (the World Self). Jung declared that the Self was the bearer of the image of the divine in man. But he emphasized that he was speaking only of experiential observations of a psychological nature and did not wish to take a position on the question of the existence of God, which must lie outside the field of psychology. Above all, he did not want to be made the founder of a religion.

However, this should not obscure the fact that Jung was a deeply religious personality, as anyone who reads his autobiography will realize. Characteristic is his answer to the question of whether he did not believe in God. "I don't believe," Jung replied, pausing for a long time. "I know!"

Nevertheless, he was quite humble about his own "truths," so if you were to meet a Jungian who thinks he can explain everything in the world with archetypes, you should be wary.

Jung's attitude was expressed in a conversation he had with the American analytical psychologist Joseph Wheelwright[3] at the beginning of their collaboration. Jung asked Wheelwright if he was sure that he had come to the right place. He explained his question by saying that there were indeed three of them who seemed to have their share of the truth: Jung, Freud, and Adler. (Imagine if there were only three today!) "None of us," said Jung, "has it, of course. We all do what we should not do, which is to generalize from our own

---

[3] Saint George and the Dandelion, p. 97f.

psychology. In reality, our concepts are personal confessions. We have generalized and abstracted them, and we produce volumes of evidence to make it look as if we have based our ideas on an overwhelming body of evidence gathered through years of clinical experience. Don't let that fool you for a moment! These are simply personal confessions." I have also felt I had come to the right place with Jung's psychology, and that is, of course, because I am Jungian in nature.

In *Chuang Tzu*, a Taoist text from the 4th century BC, there is a short anecdote: Chuang Tzu and Hui Tzu were walking along the embankment of the Hao River when Chuang Tzu remarked, "Look how the fish are coming out and darting about! They must be enjoying themselves." Hui Tzu challenged him, saying, "You're not a fish—how can you know what fish enjoy?" Chuang Tzu replied, "And you're not me—so how do you know that I don't know what fish enjoy?" Hui Tzu responded, "True, I'm not you, so I can't know what you know. But you're certainly not a fish, so that proves you don't know what fish like." Chuang Tzu then said, "Let's return to your original question. When you asked how I knew what fish like, you implied that I did know. I understand it simply from standing here, next to the Hao River."

What I express in this book, I say "from where I stand." Everything depends on the perspective from which you view things. My hope is that others will stand beside me—and see things through this lens.

Chapter 2

The Man in the Woman: Animus

From the earliest beginnings, the little girl is contained by her mother, literally in fetal life in the womb, and well into early childhood in a figurative sense, namely by her psychic identity with her mother.

This is a fundamental condition of human life and is, therefore, archetypal in character. This period is entirely dominated by the archetype of the Great Mother.[43]

The consciousness and self of the young child are still in their infancy and develop slowly in their interaction with the mother. Even when the father is actively involved in this interaction, he will psychologically have the character of a 'mother.' Only later can she begin to perceive the father as what he is: a male being completely different from herself. This happens when the male archetype begins to awaken in the girl's own psyche.

The male is something alien and unknown to the little girl and, therefore, dangerous and scary but also fascinating and attractive. However, she has within her innate psyche a readiness to meet the male. She carries within her a primordial image of the male, what we call the *animus*. At the beginning of the little girl's development, this image is latent, almost dormant in the unconscious. But the premonitions that it is beginning to stir can come very early.

A mother has recounted her little daughter's very first dream, which seems to be about this very thing. The girl was then one year and nine months old and woke up in the middle of the night crying a little. The mother says:

"I comforted her, and half asleep, she said:

– Gets so scared of the man!

Then she slept on. Now, my curiosity was aroused anyway, so the next morning, when I was changing her, I asked her what she had dreamt about during the night. A little surprisingly, she answered:

– Played ball in the garden with grandma.

---

[4] See Neumann: The Child.

Well, I said, what about the man?

– The man lies in the grass and sleeps.

I kept going: But then what happened?

My daughter reacted with a little squeal, wrapped her arms around my neck, and exclaimed:

I will be so scared if the man wakes up!

This dream has a purely archetypal character. This is often observed in the dreams of young children. The small child does not have a lot of personal, conscious experience to draw on as the adult does. This whole huge development that takes place in early childhood is, to a very large extent, controlled by the unconscious. The child is both physically and psychologically "programmed" to live in human society, and the whole development towards a personality can be described as an "awakening" rather than a mere "replenishment" process. Even babies are little personalities in their infancy; any pair of parents can recognize by the simple observation that their children are different right from the start.

Once the child has learned to walk and has also begun to speak, it enters into a loving relationship with the whole world. Everything is new and exciting and shines in marvelous light as if the world had been created in the child's honor. This is what it was like for this little girl at the time of her dream.

It was summer, and she had also, in real life, played ball with her grandmother in the garden for the very first time. So, for her, it was not something banal, everyday-like, as it would be for an adult. But back then, there was certainly no man sleeping in the grass in the real world. Thus, if we want to understand this dream properly, we need to look at the symbolic meaning of each statement. The *garden* is the scene of events. It has a maternal character as a sheltered, fertile place where all plants grow out of the earth's labouring womb. Like the Garden of Eden, it represents a primordial psychic state in which every child begins. It is a state of undifferentiated unity, which is also expressed in the myth of Adam and Eve, who happily and unconsciously went about playfully naming everything. It is also what the child does when it learns about things in the world: it names them.

Mother's *mother* is called "Grandmother" in English, and it is true that even in adult dreams, the grandmother is often more suitable than the personal mother to represent the archetypal Great Mother because she is more distant from the child than the personal mother.

The ball itself, with its round, closed shape, symbolizes totality and unity. The *game of ball* is a very apt image of the interaction between the maternal principal and the child; it is in this interaction that the child's development takes place.

In one of Grimm's fairy tales, the little princess drops her precious golden ball down a well. The ugly frog promises to pick it up if she promises to take the frog to the castle, let it eat from her plate and sleep in her bed. The princess promises and gets her ball back. But she immediately tries to renege on her promise because she thinks the frog is ugly and disgusting. But her father, the king, orders her to keep her promises.

Finally, when the frog wants to join her in her bed, it is too much for her, and she angrily throws it away. But then she is moved with compassion and runs to kiss and comfort the frog. Immediately, he turns into the most marvellous prince, with whom she can celebrate her wedding in joy and happiness.

Of course, we don't get that far in this dream. The man is asleep in the grass, and the girl is afraid that he will wake up. The first premonition that the masculine is beginning to stir in the girl's unconscious psyche comes here in the form of anxiety. This is equivalent to the little princess perceiving the prince as a nasty frog with whom she would rather not have anything to do.

It is natural that the incipient awakening of the masculine in the girl is accompanied by anxiety. For anxiety – when it does not become too overwhelming – strengthens consciousness. It strengthens the infant self, which then gradually becomes able to accept what is coming and what is inevitable. Every development has its stages, from fear to acceptance – even in adult life.

Now, if the parents have a good and warm relationship and the mother has realized her own animus to some extent, there is every chance that development will proceed in quite a natural and uncomplicated manner.

But in the real world, unfortunately, it is often the case that such favourable conditions have not been present. In the analytical work with women, animus complications play a very important role. It is not uncommon to find that women have not even completed the first phase of animus development. The male is still, in a sense, "an ugly frog." The woman has never really accepted the male on its own terms and therefore cannot establish a fully satisfactory relationship with a person of the opposite sex.

When dealing with such a problem, one must, of course, look at the personal side of the case and the nature of the relationship with the parents. But at the same time, we are already touching on a collective problem. Fathers and mothers are not unaffected by the currents of the times, nor are they unaffected by the deeper currents of the collective unconscious. Jung has said that every neurosis carries a germ of the future and that it is a price an individual pay either for not being adapted to circumstances – or for not being adapted to himself.

In an era of great change, many people become neurotic by not realizing – in a way through no fault of their own – the changes that have already taken place deep down in their psyche. They try to hold on to the traditional way where tradition no longer suffices. This is very much the case with the animus problems of the modern woman.

Just a few generations ago, among our grandmothers, women were not at all expected to realize the aspects of themselves that were traditionally considered male. It is true that ideas about women's emancipation and equality were already stirring at the beginning of the century, but it was small-scale, and the post-war period even brought a distinctly reactionary wave. In many cases, this meant that the women who had children in their forties and fifties consciously tried to live up to the traditional ideals of women as good mothers and housewives – but they neglected to realize themselves as persons.

However, I am convinced that the first wave of women's liberation lived on in the unconscious and, therefore, also strengthened the animus of the mothers' generation via the unconscious. Although it didn't look like it on the surface, in reality, patriarchy was being undermined from within. Fathers were away from home, and in many cases, it was the mother's animus that ruled the home, only with the father as the overriding figure of terror.

I don't think it's a coincidence that it was the daughters of this generation who really kick-started the women's movement, rebelling against traditional gender roles and the values of patriarchy itself. Indeed, there have been real changes in society in terms of women's equality with men that our foremothers could only dream of. In principle, the modern woman has the opportunity to realize herself in a way that was unthinkable in the past. But there is still a long way to go before women really get to know their inner man, their animus.

The woman's traditional way of dealing with her animus is projection: seeing qualities and possibilities in the man that she herself should do something to realize. A projection is, by definition, unconscious; it really looks to her as if it is the other person who has these qualities. The woman with the perhaps lesser, but to her important, talent for painting marries a painter – and then stops painting herself but instead supports him in his endeavours. Such a projection may well last a lifetime, and both parties could be satisfied on the whole. It only becomes problematic when, for one reason or another, it becomes necessary for the woman herself to withdraw the projection. This may be due to external or internal necessity, and the process usually leads to a crisis, perhaps divorce, in relation to the partner.

If the woman *fails* to project her positive animus onto her partner – or other male objects – it does not automatically mean that she realizes its possibilities herself. More often, what happens is that the psychic energy bound up in the animus becomes so strong that it occupies the ego-consciousness. The woman will then be more or less identified with her animus. This will create conflict or neurosis. Because it is an unconscious identification, it is mainly the negative side of the animus that becomes predominant. Typical effects are rigidity, emotional coldness, pessimism, self-destructiveness, opinionatedness, obstinacy, uncontrolled outbursts of affect, problems with personal relationships, especially in choosing a partner, and frequently various sexual disturbances. These may be, for example, orgasm problems, or an otherwise typically male split in sexuality and emotions, or homosexuality in an attempt to find the missing femininity there. All these problems are encountered in the analytical consulting room, and in order to turn the negative effects into something positive, a much deeper self-understanding is needed. Here, I will give an account of the preconditions and forms of transformation of the animus image in the female psyche, both archetypally, personally, and in an individual dream sequence in an individuation process.

The General Factors Shaping the Animus

There are at least four different 'building blocks' which together form the image of animus in women.

Firstly – but least importantly in our context – there is a biological duality of sex in women. The clitoris is a rudimentary penis. There are also male sex hormones in the woman. The exact connection between body and soul is, of course, completely unclear, but it must be assumed that the biological basis and genetic inheritance play a role.

Secondly, there is the archetype itself. That is, the inherent structure of the psyche that makes the woman prepared from the outset to meet the man. Fundamentally, the archetype is responsible for maintaining the attraction between the sexes. In so doing, it ensures the continuation of humankind. It is at this basic level that the link between the biological instinctual and the archetypal must be found. Even the higher apes are, to some extent, selective in their choice of mates. We can surmise that even our very early forefathers and foremothers had a kind of "guiding inner principle" that could help them not only reproduce but also select the "best" mate for the circumstances. Nowadays, it is a typical animus complication that a woman has precisely no sense of choosing a man who suits her, even when such a possibility might be at hand.

Thirdly, there is a historical factor. This is the weightiest. It is the way in which different societies have always "filled in" the basic archetypal structure with archetypal *images* of the opposite sex. These images can be reactivated at any time in the psyche of the individual woman and are as richly faceted as the different male roles and ideals throughout the ages. We encounter these images in myths and fairy tales, as well as in fiction and poetry – and we encounter them in the dreams and fantasies of modern women.

In women, the positive animus can appear as, for example, the hero, the prince, the king, the artist, the divine lover, the wise man, etc. The animus can, of course, also appear in negative form as the villain, the wretched beggar, the charlatan, the rapist, the faithless lover, the black magician.

Fourthly, there are the people the woman meets in the external world. All these actual, real men from the family and society do their part to shape the woman's animus.

First of all, of course, it is the father who plays the paramount role. We could say that he is the first carrier of the girl's animus. When she is young, she does not see him realistically but through an archetypal projection. He is the great father, a king and a sage. Only gradually does he acquire human proportions, and this development naturally influences the way in which the girl later enters into personal relationships with other men. But the archetypal image can still be projected onto other men who wear the father's mantle, so to speak. There are, for example, the teachers and bosses with whom the young woman comes into contact, and there are the more collective leaders, such as politicians and spiritual leaders, all men who possess some form of authority. The less the woman herself realizes her personal animus, the more she will submit to such authority, either by humbly bowing to it or, conversely, by being in a constant state of rebellion against anything that smacks male authority.

There is one group of men who are particularly good projectors – the *idols* we meet on stage, on television, and on the cinema screen. They are perceived as almost divine, and their worshippers can hardly imagine that they also have ordinary daily lives with ordinary problems. A star like Elvis Presley (the king) was a living myth, a collective projection of the divine lover. His "magical" charisma drew on the archetypal image. His early and rather pathetic death might say something about how dearly a person pays to identify with an archetype.

Because no real human being can conceivably fill an archetype! In more normal cases, reality steps in as a corrective. And yet, every time a woman falls deeply in love with a man, an archetypal image appears. This is what makes us see the beloved in a transfigured light, in an ideal form. Later, he begins to emerge in his more human form, with flaws and limitations.

Then we say we have withdrawn the projections. All too often, infatuation takes a turn at the same time, and the relationship gets stuck in routine and habit. This is certainly no solution! The nature of love holds far greater mysteries, for in the clarity of falling in love, we not only see our own unrealized values in projected form – we also (sometimes) see his real possibilities. The difficult balance is to keep seeing what we once saw in each other while also looking realistically at the person of the beloved. Were there no truth in this, it would be difficult to explain that love has often inspired people to do the greatest things. To move forward, we all need someone to see in us what we are not yet.

Parents and Men

In every woman's life, her parents, their relationship with her as a child, and their relationship with each other play a major role. The traditional division of roles between parents, where the father has been the provider and the mother the carer, does not always mean that the man has been the strong one and the woman the weak one in their relationship. A child naturally experiences the psychological distribution of power from the inside, and it may well turn out that the mother has been the strong and dominant one in the relationship. If the mother's animus has been unconscious and, therefore, completely archaic, and the father cannot stand up to it, the daughter's experience of the male will be strongly colored by the mother's animus.

This combination of a dominant mother and a weak father has a highly provocative effect on the daughter's animus development. She does not receive a positive female identification model through her mother but comes to identify with her animus – or her mother's animus. There are at least two typical outcomes of this combination, which mostly depend on whether the daughter reacts in an introverted or extroverted way.

In the introverted case, the daughter will typically react by being outwardly passive and compliant toward her mother in a manner similar to the father's reaction toward his wife. The aggression is turned inwards against herself in the form of an animus perfectionism, which, of course, she constantly finds she cannot live up to. The "messages" she receives from her mother are twofold: "You must get an education so that you can manage on your own," on the one hand, and "So that you don't have to succumb to men, as I have had to do. Look how much I have sacrificed for you.

You must take revenge on my behalf," on the other. The daughter is expected to live up to the ambitions that the mother was unable to fulfill. At the same time, the daughter still has to fulfill the social norms of a woman's life by getting married and having children. On the one hand, such a mother will remind her daughter that: "Marriage is not a life insurance policy," but at the same time, she is conveying the other message: "But make yourself so attractive that you can get and keep a decent man, better than the one I have. Sex may be a mess, but it's your means of power." The daughter will attempt the impossible: to simultaneously fulfill the traditional passive female role and do everything perfectly so that she can somehow win over her mother. In her relationships with men, she will often look for a soft, sensitive man, an anima-dominated man like her father. She doesn't really appreciate the male part of a man, so she often ends up being the dominant one in a relationship, just like her mother was. At the same time, she will despise the man for his weakness.

If the daughter's reaction to a domineering mother is more extroverted, she will openly try to take up the fight with her mother. Her motto could be Anything, as long as it's not like Mum!

Her animus becomes outgoing and aggressive; she will easily assume a role towards men, as in "Annie, get your gun": I can do anything better than you! In other words, her relations with men will be characterized by a competitive relationship. Her matriarchal psychological background might lead her into the more militant part of the women's movement.

Since she has had no positive female identification model, her emotional life takes a back seat; on the eros side, she is shy and vulnerable, fearful of close emotional ties. As a result of this conflict, her sexuality is often split off from the eros side, as is so often seen in men. She decides in her head that she will not enter an oppressive relationship in any case but prefers to live with loose relationships, and she does so without realizing what she is doing to her emotional life at the same time. In fact, she protects her vulnerability by lashing out violently at men who threaten to get too close to her. She might, therefore, also prefer a companionate marriage where no deeper erotic feelings are at stake. But her urge to compete with the man will be a constant problem here, too.

The opposite parental constellation – between a weak mother and a dominant father – also has two typical effects on the daughter's animus. In both cases, the animus is projected onto the father.

In the more introverted case, the daughter will try to fulfill the father's expectations of how she should be. Such a father's expectations of his daughter will often be the exact opposite of what he expects from his wife. The wife takes care of the maternal side of his anima, while the daughter must fulfill the more intellectual and spiritual side, quite unconsciously for him, of course. She tries to be the obedient, skillful pupil, always aware of what the authorities might want from her, while never asking herself what she herself really wants and is capable of. Her ego strength is not properly developed; her animus attacks her from within whenever she tries to deviate from her father's norms. Her femininity is weak and helpless like her mother's, so she will attach herself to men who are an authority to her and then try to fill her personality with their expectations of her. She tries to stay in the role of the eternal father's daughter.

In the second case, where she reacts more extraverted, she rather assumes the role of the father's "son." She identifies with her father and tries to become like him: strong, fearless, and dominant. This is the type of woman who pursues a career on men's terms and is often labeled a mannish woman.

Women's liberation and the like do not mean much to her; she, of all people, never sees herself as "oppressed," and her more feminine sisters are easily perceived as weak and stupid. In her relations with men, she frequently acts like a queen whose prince consort must walk three steps behind her. She treats men as her father treated her mother. That is, with a contempt that, on the day her husband finally rebels, gives her the surprise of her life.

These four patterns are, of course, described as extreme cases, but any reader will recognize some of them. In practice, the development of animus in a woman will be characterized by the mother's animus as well as by the fathers. Behind much of a woman's anger towards her father and men in general, there is usually something to do with the mother's animus. Since her animus has often been unconsciously mediated in the form of collective opinions and prejudices, it is this part of the animus that psychologically bridges the gap from the deeper layers of the psyche to the collective unconscious. No development of the animus is complete until it has approached a detachment from identification with the collective norms, inside and outside.

Often, the signs of the first personal animus problems in the young woman appear when she begins to fall in love with men. If the animus has been negatively shaped through her development, the projection of the animus in love cannot take place in earnest. The projection at this stage "should" actually take place as an expression of the fact that the woman is female and the man male. It also means that the girl has established a basic identification with her own sex so that she is ready to face what is different.

Unhappy infatuations are, of course, almost inevitable in the young age group. They have their own secret fascination and are, in a way, a preparation, or a prelude, to a real relationship. But if it continues well into adulthood and starts to form a pattern, you can safely look for an animus problem! There are several recognizable patterns in this: the woman finds herself falling in love repeatedly with a man who doesn't want her. This may be because he is always already married or because he is otherwise unattainable. He may not be interested at all, or he may have a similar problem to herself, so she always falls for an immature man who can never really commit to any woman and therefore may want to have a relationship with her – but always with a certain emotional distance.

Of course, she can't understand it herself! Why does it always have to happen to her? But if she gradually learns to look inside herself, she will realize that it is a "fantasy lover" at work. She spends her emotional life daydreaming about how wonderful she and he could be together – if only... She waits and waits and waits. But one day, she might turn the question on its head and ask herself, does she even want him?

Another variation of the negative animus is that the woman may be in a committed relationship but not an equal one. She may find herself with a man who she feels oppresses and dominates her and prevents her from realizing herself. Or conversely, she may find herself a wimp of a man whom she then oppresses and dominates. Often, her animus will tell her that it is indeed all her own fault, she is hopelessly impossible – or she projects the problem onto him and does not see her own part at all.

The woman who more smoothly projects her positive animus onto a suitable partner has children with him, and lives in a reasonably good marriage will often only be confronted with her animus at a more mature age, more specifically, when the children have grown up and left home. Then, the question naturally arises as to what she is in herself and what she wants to do with the rest of her life. "Menopause" has long been used as an excuse to explain away this perfectly normal life crisis in women. Only in a few cases are the disturbances rooted in hormonal changes, so that it is these that produce the troublesome symptoms. Two other factors are more important. Firstly, the changed social situation itself, and secondly, the corresponding psychological situation. The energy that the woman has hitherto invested in the home and children sinks into the unconscious and constellates the animus. If the woman is not prepared to make some changes in her life and fill it with a different kind of meaning, she will have problems. The animus energy that is not used constructively occupies the consciousness and can also cause physical symptoms such as headaches, dizziness, breathing problems, visual disturbances, outbursts of rage alternating with depressive moods, and perhaps even psychotic outbursts. Animus seems to be physically associated with the head and the respiratory system.

It is probably fair to say that it has been most 'natural' for women to develop their masculine aspects in the second half of their lives. In many primitive societies, it has been observed that women change their status after menopause and can take up otherwise male positions that are excluded for women of childbearing age.

But we no longer live in a primitive society, and the development of culture, as well as the corresponding development of the collective unconscious, seems to have meant that the problem of animus in modern women is more urgent than ever before and generally appears earlier in life than before. Culture modifies nature, and I believe that today, it is natural for women to develop their masculine sides.

It seems to me that reality speaks for itself: If a woman is stuck in the old gender roles and at the same time has an extensive animus disposition, she becomes neurotic. But we are living in a time of transition, where the new is still in its infancy. It is not easy for the woman because, to the extent that she takes on this spiritual task, she is making history. She is changing traditions and norms; she is actually creating culture.

The difficulty of this task should not be underestimated. Changing centuries of cultural norms is a difficult and dangerous heroic endeavor that has hitherto been the privilege and responsibility of men. At the same time, as there is a trend in the psyche towards greater awareness, there is also a marked inertia. The desire to bring to light what has hitherto been unconscious is not without cost. When Prometheus stole fire from the gods, he was severely punished. Now that female Prometheus wants to steal the light of consciousness, they too are in a perilous situation. The first women's liberation activists had to make huge personal sacrifices. In the beginning, the price was their entire feminine side: erotic love, marriage, children, and home. Nowadays, the high divorce rate speaks for itself. But time is more with women now: A fusion of the male and the female in the woman (and in the man) could possibly take place.

Female Psychological Development

The analytical psychologist Erich Neumann has described the different phases of women's psychological development as seven stages:[5]

1. Self-conservation phase
2. The invasion of the patriarchal Uroboros
3. The phase of self-surrender
4. Captivity in the patriarchal Uroboros
5. Encountering the male
6. The phase of surrender and devotion to the Self
7. Discovery of the Self.

In the following, I will explain how the development of animus generally takes place in these phases and how the attachment to one of these phases binds the woman's animus to certain ways of experiencing the male and men.

The phase of self-conservation usually lasts for the first few years of the girl's life and goes back into the pre-natal state. As I described in my discussion of the little girl's dream, the animus here is in a completely unconscious state. If the adult woman remains bound to this phase, it can be said of her that she is fully woman but only half human. She will be incapable of recognizing any values other than those of a woman, and when she comes into contact with a partner, her relationship with him will be characterized mainly by the basic biological relationships: he will have to bear her children and bring home the food. But who he is as a person and as a man is of little interest to her. Her unconscious animus holds both husband and children in an iron grip. No one gets away with her goodwill!

---

[5] On the psychology of the female.

Whether she dominates overtly as the matriarch of the family or indirectly through weakness and helplessness is a matter of her personal disposition and environmental factors.

The invasion of the patriarchal Uroboros usually takes place between the ages of 3-6 years. This is the animus awakening in its all-encompassing form as the male part of the Self. For the girl, this is a numinous experience, accompanied by both fear and fascination. She experiences it as an intrusion into her psyche of something violent and overwhelming. An attachment to this phase can result in either a deep fear of the later sexual male intrusion or a great – perhaps too great – fascination with the male, which creates the basis for a later animus obsession of the consciousness. It is the intrusion of the archetype that is responsible for the little girl's pronounced seductive behavior towards her father at this age. The animus is usually projected onto the father. It is by no means just a matter of childish sexuality. The girl's first experience of the other sex is a holistic experience in which spirit and sexuality are not differentiated, just as it can be seen that in 'primitive' religions, there is no contradiction between these two entities.

This is the reason for the woman's indisputably greater ability than the man to experience the spiritual/ religious in unity with the sexual/erotic. It is not unusual for a woman to respond erotically, even with orgasm, e.g., through intense listening to music or a spiritually riveting conversation. Every revivalist preacher, or rock star for that matter, plays consciously on the power of the spirit and music to bring women into an ecstatic state.

Attachment to this phase enables the woman to encounter the male in an ecstatic-orgiastic way but not to encounter the man as an equal partner. What fascinates her is the strange, the unknown, the overwhelming, in an impersonal male form. The girl still lives in a fundamentally matriarchal state. In adult women's dreams, this intrusion of the male is reflected in the very common dream of the stranger entering, usually accompanied by fear, anxiety, but also fascination. Many women's sexual fantasies involve a stranger – or a whole group of anonymous men – taking her by force, but this is accompanied by lust. Often these fantasies are followed by a sense of shame; in real life, the woman would not want to be raped in any way. The fascination lies in the overwhelming masculinity, which the woman ecstatically accepts.

In ancient Babylon, the temples of the great goddess Ishtar were associated with sacred harlots. But it was also customary that every young woman had to go to the temple and give herself to the first stranger who asked her to do so. Only then could she marry. The psychological significance of this seems to be – contrary to our understanding – that the woman had to make a sacrifice to the goddess of love and impersonal sexual power before she could allow herself to commit herself to a man. Of course, it makes no sense to speak of binding to a phase in this context, as it was a respectable cultural trait.

In the next phase, *the phase of self-surrender,* the girl will leave the matriarchal primordial ground and accept the masculine values. This takes place in our schooling. The way it is taught and what is emphasized is masculine values. Paradoxically, the girls are finding it easier to conform to and acquire the school curriculum neatly and politely. But this is precisely because, for girls, it is not a question of identity but of projection. The animus is projected partly onto the father and partly onto the teachers at school as objects of love, and they, therefore, accept what is demanded more readily than the boys. Already here, however, a difference in the dispositions of the girls can be seen. Many girls really only accept the masculine at face value; the center of gravity of their world remains feminine. I remember when I was at school, one of my female friends divided the girls in our class into two groups: One group was the 'ladies' – already in pre-puberty, extremely feminine in their entire appearance, while the other group was the 'trouser-girls' (tomboys) – at that time trousers were not as common as they are now. Several of us in the trouser-girl group had never been particularly interested in girls' games, preferring to participate in boys' activities, which we found more exciting. These were undoubtedly girls with a greater animus facility and with a greater degree of identification with the animus. Since gender identity is generally somewhat fluid until puberty, this rarely creates major problems for the girl unless the environment already then takes a reproachful and restrictive approach to "tomboys." After all, a wide margin is allowed for pre-pubescent girls. With the onset of puberty, however, a problem arises. It coincides, I believe, with the phase that Neumann calls *Captivity in the patriarchal Uroboros.*

It becomes necessary for the girl to divide the world into genders. She must establish her own gender identity and can no longer delude herself that she is a dual-gendered being. The transformation that takes place on a physical level, with girls becoming women and boys becoming men, is accompanied by equally profound changes on an inner level.

Now, it becomes paramount for the girl to find out what it means to be a woman. One of the problems is that this is largely determined by a male society's norms about what is feminine and what is not. The girl will usually try to identify with the prevalent feminine ideals, and she will reject in herself what appears to her to be masculine. She undertakes a gender polarisation.

It is well known that at this point, girls' intellectual achievements decline, and boys overtake them. With the first crushes, girls begin to project animus onto boys rather than onto father figures and concentrate on impressing them. I think many women who have tried to teach their girls about other kinds of feminine roles are shocked when they suddenly realize that their daughters still fall into the role of the one who must please the boys.

For those girls who have an extensive animus disposition, provoked by their upbringing and environment or as a natural predisposition, the development process is more complex than for the more feminine girls. They easily become very divided because, on the one hand, they have a strong subjective need to continue to develop their "masculine" sides, but on the other hand, they have an equally strong need to become women. As their feminine side is relatively less developed than that of many of their sisters, these girls will often use the most exaggerated means to attract attention, lots of make-up, and provocative clothing. The less secure the girl is in her feminine gender identity, the more she has to reassure herself that others – especially men – see her as a woman.

Quite common to the problems of the modern woman is the partial identification with the animus. As I said, this happens easily during puberty if a workable balance between the male and female sides of the psyche cannot be found. I mentioned the division of "trouser girls" and "ladies" in my own class at school. Now, I don't know what happened to the other "trouser girls," but for my own part, the development of animus was not without problems.

From secondary school onwards, I felt violently torn between my intellectual and spiritual side – and the side that could make it with the other young people, especially the boys. There was no room for all of me in the role I had to play to be accepted, so I had a secret spiritual life!

It consisted, among other things, of a series of written fantasies, the psychological significance of which I had not the faintest idea of at the age of 15 or 16. I myself thought it was art!
The first major story reads:

> I heard music. Faintly, but clearly. I didn't know where I was or what I was, but the music led me to a lonely beach. And the beach was white and grey, and the sea was unhappy and roaring in its mournful rhythm, the sky was crying silently. The tears flowed in unison with the sea and made little holes in the sand. I walked slowly and lingeringly with my feet on the water's edge, and my heart was a stone in my stomach. But I was a little happy because there is more happiness in pain than in indifference.
>
> How deserted it was. Not even any birds. Then, I dug a hole in the sand and stood down there. When I had patted the sand well together, only my head and arms protruded above. I stood there for a long time,

feeling protected and almost content. The water from above wet my hair and made it drip from my nose.

I dug myself free again. It was much harder than it had been to get down there, and I wished I had never made that hole. But I had to go up because there was something I was looking for. Yet it seemed to me to be something fundamental, something I had once had but had lost before I came here. It was like having forgotten a wonderful dream. And knowing that I had dreamt, it was enough to make all my soul's desire to find it again. For an eternity, I searched everywhere, everywhere.

Then I saw something dark out on the water. Gradually, I realized that it was a tree trunk on which someone was sitting, and the beach, the music of my world, once again emerged from the depths of my consciousness. I waved and shouted, ran back and forth, seized by a marvelous eagerness. But my voice did not reach my lips, and my movements were just like those peculiar to the nightmare. I was not noticed at all, yet I kept running back and forth, gesticulating and screaming, hoping to make contact with him out there on the tree trunk.

For it was indeed his music that had brought me here. His intense playing with that saxophone, which so obviously stole all his attention, had brought me to this life, this consciousness. There was no doubt about it; I had always known it and had only remembered it anew when I saw him playing his saxophone.

And therefore, he had to be able to see me, to hear me. In my joy and eagerness, I rushed into the water to reach him faster. I swam and swam, trying all the time to wave and shout, but I slipped under the surface of the water each time. And although I kept getting closer, he was getting harder to reach, and he still did not see me but continued his music.

I could now hear the music only in fragments, for the sea lapped and drowned out its frail rival, but now and then, the beautiful notes reached me and revitalized me.

To reach him was essential. And yet, it seemed impossible. Like the rainbow, he fled without moving and without taking any notice of me. He had created all this and me, and yet – or because of that – he could not see me.

It was completely useless, and I was very tired, but I could not stop swimming. Then the music got weaker. Finally, I could not even hear it anymore, even though his face was very concentrated. I was extremely tired, and the water was as soft as a duvet. A little later, I saw him drifting or fading away, dissolving into a cloud of bubbles.

The water was bright and welcomed me gently. But it was so quiet, no music at all – and down below, there was nothing at all. As the very last thing, I recognized only the illusion and, behind it, endless, rumbling laughter that filled me with sleepy contentment and a strange, recognizable joy.

Needless to say, at that age, I had no way of understanding what was really going on in my unconscious, let alone relating it to a real-life problem. To make sense of this fantasy and understand its various symbolic details, I shall try to systematize the events.

The girl on the beach. This is the scene of events and is described as an inner symbolic landscape; the sea is "unhappy," and the sky is "weeping." Now, of course, this could be seen as an expression of a typical adolescent mood. But the beach and the sea are also a classic image of the unconscious meeting consciousness. The basic mood is thus mournful and lonely.

The hole in the sand. The girl digs herself in and feels a little protected. Symbolically, of course, this corresponds to shutting oneself in, hiding. But then the fantasy develops itself; the narrator wants to go further and search for a deeper cause of the emotional climate.

The cause of the music now heard again, turns out to be a man sitting on a tree trunk on the water, playing the saxophone. It becomes clear that this world of souls was created by him: "he had created all this and me."

In many ways, this male figure epitomizes the animus in its archetypal form. He is a musician; he is a world and consciousness-raiser, and he's sitting on a log. It is not a ship or even a dinghy; he is sitting astride a tree trunk. It is impossible to miss the phallic symbolism, which is also reflected in the choice of instrument – the saxophone.

It is not unknown that musicians have a special attraction for women. Music is probably the art form that most clearly links the spiritual with the erotic, and there are probably not a few women who have made the mistake of thinking that the man who played or sang so marvelously must also be a divine lover. Here, the animus plays a trick on them. My grandmother used to say that she fell in love with her first husband just because he played the piano so beautifully. Somewhat cynically, she went on to say that if he had not died, they would probably have divorced because there was not much else about him.

But this animus is further combined with the creative principle. He is the creator of consciousness. Here, we see him swimming in the sea of the collective unconscious, a personification of the unconscious, so to speak. This is the position of the animus; he is the one who conveys ideas of the unconscious to the woman, and he is the bearer of the creative impulse. It has been said so often that women are very seldom as creative as men are – and this is partly connected with the fact that the animus has very seldom had the opportunity of really entering into contact with the woman's consciousness.

For this inner connection to be fruitful, it must be an eros connection. The girl somehow realizes this and throws herself straight into the waves. This shows the problem of the unconscious and the very problematic outcome of fantasy. She does not succeed since he does not see her at all, and she sinks to the bottom of the sea.

Now, what does this mean psychologically? There seems to be a problem with the very way animus is described: he is only concerned with himself and his music. He is closed in; he is auto-erotic. I told you before that my spiritual life at that time was "secret," almost in the same way that in the past, one could speak of a "secret" sexual life, which usually meant indulging in the dreadful practice of masturbation. But I was quite openly preoccupied with eroticism and boys, and neither then nor later was sexuality a problem in itself.

So, there are two sides to phallic symbolism, both sexual and spiritual – and one must be careful not to automatically focus on the sexual side whenever phallic motifs appear. It may well be, as in my case, that the problem is how to put one's creative abilities into practice; how to give the spiritual animus a place in actual life?

Here, at any rate, it does not succeed. The ego is lost in the sea of the unconscious. Such an outcome is, of course, not harmless. It is this kind of drowning of the ego that happens in psychoses. But where the ego is stronger, only a partial "drowning" occurs. Psychologically, this corresponds to an animus obsession. The ego identifies itself more or less totally with the animus. That is what happened here. From then on, almost all the following stories or fantasies that I wrote down were told with a male "I." It is not so rare for a woman to dream that she is a man. It is an unmistakable sign of an animus identification.

Such a problem affects the choice of partner, as I mentioned earlier: no permanent relationship is established, or the relationships that are established are characterised by a mutually negative symbiosis, with each party locking the other in with their own unresolved problems. This means that the fifth psychological stage cannot be reached. This is what Neumann calls *Encountering the Male* or the patriarchal marriage. The possibility of this phase is very much reflected in the young girl's – or indeed the adult woman's – daydreams of the prince on the white horse who comes to take her to the castle.

There are many folk tales about how the woman is prepared for this encounter. This also happens in the fairy tale "The Ditch." It is about the haughty princess who rejects all suitors because she finds fault with all of them. This is how we can recognize the negative animus! The last one, a king's son, is rejected because his chin is too crooked. Her father grows tired of her stubbornness and proclaims that he will give her to the first person who turns up, whoever he is. A miserable beggar comes along and takes her as his wife. She is kindly allowed to accompany him to his poor hut; she is put to work making clay pots and selling them by the roadside. She is also put on kitchen duty at the palace, where preparations are being made for the wedding of the king's son. The point is that when she finally overcomes her pride and learns to love her harsh beggar husband, it turns out that he was really the king's son in disguise, and the wedding can then be celebrated with joy.

Psychologically, this is about a girl with a negative animus – and how to tame it. In the fairy tales, this is a rather tangible matter, and in order not to provoke the animus of my female readers unnecessarily, I should immediately hasten to say that it is, of course, also about the collective psyche – that is, the patriarchal society's – way of dealing with things. The story does not say anything about whether she will later be able to use her animus in a positive way.

It could be said that the wisdom of the collective psyche, as expressed in the fairy tales, leads the woman up to and through precisely this fifth phase, the encounter with the man, the 'prince,' where she becomes able to encounter the man as a man at all, erotically and spiritually. The classic Freudian analysis did not go any further but characterized the whole problem as 'penis envy,' pure and simple. A woman is a woman, and she must accept that!

But the evolution of the modern woman leads her out of patriarchal psychology and into a *process of individuation*. There are two main phases in this process. One is *the surrender and devotion to the Self*, in which the woman meets her "prince" on the inner level, that is, integrates her animus. She will then be able to realize her spiritual and creative possibilities directly and independently of male values. At the same time, such a process will mean that most projections will fall away from the partner so that she will be able to see his real being.

But what about love, some might ask, does it disappear? Well, the infatuation that can only thrive in dim lighting, of course, disappears when you draw the curtains and can see clearly who is in front of you. Those who are afraid to put it to the test may already have an inkling of the outcome. This is one of the typical obstacles to the development of consciousness. It is not only she who will see him more clearly. She herself becomes more "visible" because awareness provides clearer personality boundaries, and she may also risk becoming less attractive in her partner's eyes. It is incredibly difficult for a woman to show her lover her true colors, but that is what she must do.

The second phase of individuation is the *phase of discovery of the Self,* 'Selbst-findung,' as Neumann calls it. For the woman, the encounter with the Self is naturally female in character. I shall go into these phases in more detail in the chapter on "the individuation of the female." Here, I shall only mention that the various phases are by no means covered once and for all, but that they are, so to speak, repeated at every stage of development and that they are thus also gone through in the individuation process.

Recently, I had a conversation with a friend. She told me that she had been thinking a lot about the roles of women in trivial literature. She had recently read the old bestseller "Amber Always Amber" (by K. Winsor), which is about a beautiful, red-haired, passionate woman who is, however, utterly amoral and destructive in her attempt to gain power and influence through her gender. She becomes, i.a., the king's mistress. The only person she is in love with is a black-haired hero whom she will do anything to win. His feelings for her are lust, but the woman he loves and marries is a young woman of a good family – which Amber is not – and his wife is, of course, Amber's absolute opposite: gifted, good, and noble. Amber is portrayed in the novel in an entirely negative light. Now my friend had thought that this novel, written by a male author, represented the male division of women into the passionate whore and the pure and noble Madonna. But then she realized that a similar division actually existed in, e.g., Barbara Cartland's novels, which millions of women devour. She herself had been mesmerized by them at times. Here, the heroine is always the good woman who falls in love with the handsome hero with the bad reputation and some Amber-like mistress. However, he turns out to be noble to the core, abandons his mistress, and encloses the heroine in his strong embrace. So, the same pattern seemed to correspond in some way to something in women that perhaps went deeper than that. But how could this be related to a modern female consciousness?

The next day, she called me and told me that she had had a dream that had made a strong impression on her. It was undoubtedly related to what we had been talking about:

Together with some other women, I am sailing to an island. Soon after we have come ashore, we are attacked and captured by some men. I am taken into a room where the leader is present, a tall, black-haired, broad-shouldered man. He sits on a wide bed where a woman is sprawling provocatively. She has reddish hair and is wearing a semi-transparent black negligee-like dress. I am placed elsewhere on the bed. Something is going on between the two of them; he lifts her up as if embracing her but then suddenly puts his arm around her neck by the throat and strangles her. I look away but half suspect that a similar fate is in store for me. Strangely enough, I am not particularly afraid.

Then, the black-haired man comes up to me. He looks at me; I notice that he is very attractive, a real "man." He now tells me to masturbate. I obey and become sexually aroused. Then he lays down on top of me, we have intercourse, and we both ejaculate. A little later, I asked, "Am I going to choke now, too?" No, he replies. I lean towards him and say, "Then I'll confide in you that it was nice."

Later, I walk around the neighborhood. Somehow, I learned that the red-haired woman had caused him a lot of harm over several years by somehow abusing a child they had together.

Then I'm at a party or something; the man is there too. He has the power on the island. There are other women who are obviously attracted to him, but to my surprise, I am the only one he treats with anything but courtesy. I ask him at one point what has become of the other women who were also captured. He explains that there has been a misunderstanding. His men were not sure of which of the women was me and thus captured them all. They will be released immediately. Finally, I realize that there are no limits to my own freedom either. The only constraints he has placed on me are the feelings between us. I have a strong sense of reciprocity but also of his otherness as a male.

This dream is a textbook example of living through all the stages of psychological development I have mentioned! The beginning is uncertain, but the ship that holds the women and sails across the maternal sea may represent the purely matriarchal phase, the phase of self-conservation. Immediately afterward, the assault seems to represent the Invasion of the masculine, leading to the phase of self-surrender through the initially passive role of the dreamer, even to the point of resigning herself to the possible 'death wedding.' The excessively feminine position is reflected in the role of the red-haired woman, which corresponds to the captivity in the patriarchy, where the woman is completely subordinated to the needs of the man. (She is strikingly reminiscent of Amber).

But it is precisely this passive attitude on the part of the dreamer herself that leads to the orgiastic encounter with the male: the scene is strikingly ambiguous. What, on the one hand, could be seen as a male pornographic fantasy, the woman's exhibition of herself to him, is, on the other hand, a sexual activity on the part of the dreamer herself, for she is not actually "raped" but gives herself to him.

This seems to change the whole situation since, in her relationship with the man, she has entered the phase of self-surrender, and what seemed to be a negative relationship has now dissolved into a positive one. The killing of the other woman turns out to be "just" and must be seen psychologically as a rejection of the kind of female power that the woman has exploited through her gender; the damage that both sexes suffer when Eros becomes a means of struggle and power. Surprisingly, the dark man turns out not to have harem-like tendencies, for the real reason for the dreamer's capture was that he had chosen her as his partner. He wants an equal, free relationship bound only by love.

It was this realization at the end of the dream that felt so liberating and, for my friend, provided a kind of answer to why Cartland's novels appeal so strongly to women: They touch strongly on the need for women to be psychologically chosen by their men.

What in the psychology of patriarchy becomes the woman's passive waiting for the prince has its counterpart in a psychological fact: If the man, as a man, has not chosen the woman he lives with, the relationship becomes deeply unsatisfactory for her. The fact that she is seen and loved as a person and as a woman gives her the necessary space to realize her own values. She is free to develop her relationship with both her partner in external reality and the archetypal animus in the inner world.

This is not to say, of course, that a woman cannot or should not be the active party and choose the man she wants. But her choice, if it comes first in time, must and should be followed by him deciding in the same way in favor of her. The important thing here is the psychological choice, for there are many examples of a man who, even after a marriage that may have lasted as long as a silver wedding anniversary, has still not "chosen" his wife but has remained tied to his mother.

Such relationships lock both partners in; their development is stunted. They never get beyond the conventional side of the relationship but let ordinary norms determine the framework of the relationship. The woman's more or less unconscious longing for 'something more' may then be expressed through identification with the Cartland heroines. Conscious or not, the deeply feminine in every woman can only be satisfied by the encounter with the deeply masculine in every man. In a conscious process of individuation, it is a question of the union of opposites and, as the fruit of this fusion, the realization of the *Self.*

The Animus as the Dynamic Factor in the Female Psyche

Jung conceived of the logos principle as the principle that could characterize the masculine form of consciousness. In her article on animus, Emma Jung[6] develops this idea in relation to the animus of the woman. There is a fourfold structure in the logos principle, which can be seen as a progressive succession. Each stage has simultaneous representation in life and in the development of the woman's animus when viewed dynamically.

Jung refers to these four stages as 'Power, Deed, Word, Meaning.' We can understand this as:

a. The masculine is an expression of physical strength and will.
b. The heroic masculine – the purposeful action.
c. The masculine is an expression of the clarity of the intellect and its verbal expression.
d. The masculine is an expression of the power of the spirit in a spiritual and religious sense.

All these aspects can be experienced in projected form or as expressions of the woman's own inner animus. The male is perceived as having physical power and will respond to the "primitive" in every man and woman; it is this aspect that physically draws the sexes towards each other. A woman whose animus corresponds to this stage of development will easily project her animus onto men, who in some way represent physical strength and power. Collectively, these may be sports heroes, bodybuilders, or, among film idols, those who are most notable for their physical strength and primitive male sex appeal.

---

[6] Animus and Anima, p.3

The transition to the next phase is, of course, not sharp. There are many degrees between the masculine as an expression of willpower and as an expression of purposeful action. The Greek mythological heroes are not always characterized by a pronounced ability to grasp a situation, but they act without fear or favor. Interestingly, their approach to a situation seems to be strongly linked to how they relate to women. The Iliad is about the hero Achilles' anger at having lost a slave woman, not because he loved her so much, but because it was his rightful property that was taken from him. When he finally throws himself back into the fight against the Trojans, it is to avenge the death of his friend Patroclus. He possesses enormous heroic strength; as we know, only his heels are vulnerable, but his life is that of a warrior, and his goal is an honorable death. The hero who returns home after the battle, Odysseus, on the other hand, has a very friendly relationship with women; he is described as 'cunning' and performs his heroic deeds with wisdom rather than brute strength, often with the help of various women.

The typical animus hero is thus more likely to be a romantic hero who might conceivably want to lay his victories at the feet of the lady of his heart. Collective projection figures for this animus are successful men, war heroes, pioneers, all men who perform modern heroic deeds – or portray them on the cinema screen. In the now old (but still played) film, "Gone with the Wind," this animus phase is represented by the adventurer and actor Rhett Butler.

The woman whose animus is most characterized by this hero phase will often be the typical "woman behind the man" – behind the head of some major enterprise. In this way, she indirectly fulfills her animus ambition through the man (while at the same time having her own person confirmed by being the chosen woman of the capable man). It is not uncommon to hear of a spoilt wife taking over the firm after her husband's death and suddenly displaying determination and administrative skills that no one knew she had.

Generally speaking, the modern woman is very well capable of showing power of action and working determinedly towards some overall goal she has set herself. Apart from the almost self-evident fact that the modern woman can independently manage a job, children, and everything else that is needed for life to run smoothly, I could also cite numerous current examples of active movements dominated by women. Some of the best known are "Women for Peace," the Danner Foundation, and the Joan Sisters – as well as the women's movement as a whole, of course. Here, you will find lots of women who put their energy, hard work, and sacrifice into a cause they believe in.

For a very long time in our culture, there has been a division between the work of the hand and the work of the spirit. Men have, in principle, though not always in practice, been free to choose where they wanted to place themselves. For women, the same division has been further emphasised by the traditional role of women. It is quite new that women, too, are, in principle, free to choose whether they wish to practice the work of the hand or the spirit.

As soon as we come to the question of the third phase of the animus – the male as an expression of the clarity of the intellect and its verbal expression, it generally becomes more difficult for the woman to differentiate and integrate the animus. As I mentioned in the previous section, the schoolgirl is already more inclined than the schoolboy to recognize male authority in intellectual matters.

When the adult woman wants to continue into the intellectual world, she realizes at some point that most thoughts are thought by men. Often, she will settle for that, for "truths" that have already been expressed. She will tend to adopt her husband's opinions and attitudes. In other words, she projects the intellectual part of the animus onto him.

Women's typical complaints about their difficulty in 'expressing' themselves can be interpreted as a failure to integrate animus as 'the word.' At the same time, they are all too easily impressed by men's powers of speech, which are by no means always the expression of particularly impressive thought. If the projection can hold up, things are going very well; the man and the woman each fulfill their own place in the psychic spectrum. But if the woman's own animus is actually characterized by intellectual inclinations, and she does not do the work of personally relating to the logos principle, the animus begins to function very negatively.

In relationships, there is often an unconscious competition that the man perceives as incredibly dominant. It is the woman's animus that speaks out in the discussions, and it has this perpetually criticizing character. Often, the woman herself is unhappy about this, but she is helplessly at the mercy of the animus: at the slightest challenge, she must pick on the man and find fault with everything he says and does. She becomes compulsively vindictive and must be right at all costs. But her "truths" are characterized by collective opinions and prejudices; they are only "true" in general and not necessarily in relation to this or that particular situation.

With other women, the animus is not at all provoked in the same way as it is with men, especially with their partners. This is because the woman is not alone in the game: Together with the man, she provokes his anima so that he immediately reacts with negative emotions to what she says. He becomes emotional and irritable and, like her, stops sticking to the issue at hand. Communication between the two sinks to a rather primitive level, and if there is an audience, it is usually quite clear to them what is going on: The men think, "What a battleaxe he's married to," and the woman, "he's a horrible male chauvinist." No, of course, I am putting the matter on edge. The outsiders, who are not emotionally involved, will more easily be able to see the issue from two sides and perhaps mediate.

I told you before about my own imagination from the age of 15-16 and the following unconscious animus identification. It was, of course, still there when I started in analysis some years later – and was immediately diagnosed. A few months into the analysis, I had a dream that very clearly said something about the psychic work ahead.

I have an appointment with my analyst. There are so many people all the time that I cannot get to it. There is one person in the flat in particular who keeps getting in the way: a strange male figure, shapeless like the cartoon character who appears in the advertisements for Michelin car tires. He wants to sleep with me, and I push him away in disgust. Eventually, I get to the analyst's house, who has now been replaced by his (unknown to me) wife. I tell her about the strange man out there. She explained to me that it has something to do with the method they have there on site. You sort of unravel people or rewind them, and then you build them up again. She shows me a picture, which is a kind of symbol of how far you can go with that method. As soon as she showed me the picture, it came alive like a film. It shows the young Churchill on horseback, surrounded by riders. He raises his saber and throws it into the air as if in triumph and is followed by the others. Then I left the consultation room, and in the flat, I met the strange man again. But this time, I am moved by compassion and embrace him. Then, the strange thing happens: he transforms and becomes a real human being. Eventually he becomes my brother, and we sit side by side on a couch and read a book together.

You see, the shapeless Michelin man was, of course, my own undifferentiated animus, which also stood in the way of deeper contact with the analyst. He represents the animus as a raw, unformed force, the first stage of animus development. In the advertisement, the figure appeared as a symbol of the strength of the tires and the dynamism of the car. I was at that time completely intellectually undisciplined; the energy he represents was not at all available to my consciousness. This is also shown in the dream by the fact that I want nothing to do with him.

When I finally reached the analyst, he had become a woman. This represents a deeper level of emotional contact, on the one hand, the anima of the analyst, on the other hand, a piece of unconscious femininity in myself. She explains the man to me in words that are clearly an image of the analytical process, this unraveling and subsequent construction. So, Churchill is the image of what you can achieve in the future. Strangely enough, I had no conscious experience of him as something special. In my mind, he was just an old man with a perpetual cigar in his mouth. A subsequent reading of his biography gave me a somewhat different view of the range of his personality – for better or worse. Churchill can be said to epitomize the third animus phase, which contains the first two. He was incredibly dynamic and, indeed, the great hero of the war, an excellent organizer – and, as an expression of the third animus phase, a master of words.

Of course, this does not make me a new female Churchill! But the dream did suggest that there was an animus possibility which, if integrated, could release some such qualities in myself. The saber he throws into the air is a symbol of the discernment of the logos principle; it is a striking weapon, as opposed to, say, a rapier, which is a stabbing weapon.

But there was certainly a long way to go – because the current situation had to start with the Michelin man. My attitude towards him was changed, and thus, he began to be transformed. This embrace in the dream is so characteristic of the way a woman must approach her negative animus. Unless she can perform a form of devotion, no transformation takes place. The erotic symbolism recurs even where, as here, it is a question of something intellectual rather than sexual. The man becomes the brother, and we sit reading a book, utterly chaste. The result for me was that I resumed my interrupted university education and began studying the history of religion. Suddenly, I realized that I had acquired a capacity for a self-disciplined study that I had simply never had before. The unconscious had had it.

In many other cases, however, you will find that a negative animus has not exactly affected the capacity for self-discipline. There are women who have already completed their education and are perhaps well into some kind of career but are stuck in it. Such a woman can be severely plagued by perfectionist demands from within – it's the negative animus whispering "It's not good enough! Only the perfect is good enough." The cure is the same in all cases: the woman must manage to establish an emotionally orientated attitude towards the animus. Then, there must be a realization of what this animus stands for. It is a question of finding out where in her life the woman has the possibility to make an intellectual or creative contribution. It could be, e.g., that a woman who has been propelled in a profession by an ambitious animus has neglected some minor artistic talent precisely because it was not "smart" enough. But indulging in such a practice anyway can provide an outlet for the pent-up, and therefore negative, animus energy.

Generally, the problem is that an unconscious identification with the animus causes the woman to aim too unrealistically high. She may have a head full of fantasies about creating a marvelous new philosophy, writing the book of all time, taking a new degree, or whatever. The symptom is simply that she can never get comfortable taking the first modest steps. The animus fantasy is so big, and she cannot bear to realize how far there is actually to go and that she is unlikely to achieve even a fraction of what the animus illusion pretends. But if, in all modesty, she does the work of realizing her own personal possibilities and forces her consciousness to take a personal stance on the material she is working with, the animus obsession disappears.

That is to say, the aspects of the animus that belong to the personal disposition are integrated. At the same time, the archetypal part of the animus is given its rightful place as a mediator in relation to the inner world. This part of the animus can never be exhausted because it belongs to the collective unconscious, but one can enter into an inner relationship with it. Through dreams and fantasies, it can provide the consciousness with inspirations and creative impulses – and, above all, it can provide the woman with a greater capacity to understand the opposite sex. Her tendency to project her own difficulties with animus onto the man and the world of men is considerably diminished. As true as it is that this society takes very little account of women's values, as essential it is for women to learn to distinguish between their animus anger and a criticism of the facts.

The fourth stage of animus development has to do with the spiritual and religious side of the masculine. Here, too, the great questions about the meaning of life have been answered by men. The spiritual male has a marked tendency to make all-embracing spiritual syntheses that pretend to be eternal truths of a completely objective nature. This part of the animus is almost always projected. I do not know if one can say that women have a greater religious and spiritual need than men, but in any case, one often sees the fact that around some spiritual "gurus," there are mostly women. They are usually bound not only by the spiritual theories he has but as much by their greater or lesser infatuation with him. As I have said before, it is a very basic feature of female psychology that eroticism and spirit are closely connected. Thus, if the woman projects her spiritual animus onto a man, it is almost inevitable that some part of her instinct will follow.

Such a situation places extraordinary demands on the ethical behavior of the 'guru,' and many are unable to live up to it. From the outside, such an assembly can easily look more like a powerful male baboon with a harem of females than a forum for spiritual development. In this context, the Catholic Church's requirement of celibacy for priests is a psychological safeguard, although in other ways, of course, it is precisely what prevents a synthesis of eros and spirit.

If the animus is characterized by spirit, the woman will naturally feel drawn to those places where universal questions are asked. In the past, a spiritually-minded woman went to a convent, and even the greatest female religious talents had to proceed from male premises. Lifelong celibacy must surely be a male invention; female psychology prefers to sanctify sexuality, as can be seen in the various rites of the great goddess. The man, in a patriarchal culture, came to identify himself with the supra-personal male, striving for purity of spirit separate from the instinctual bondage to the female primordial ground. At the same time, he longed so much for the paradisiac primordial unity that his consciousness had to protect itself with all sorts of prohibitions. The woman thus had to suffer this prevailing form of spirit; it proved to be stronger than the old matriarchal form of spirit, where the woman herself stood in the spiritual center and was inspired or ecstatically in contact with the suprapersonal, male spiritual principle – as a shaman, völva, sibyl, priestess.

But this ancient matriarchal mentality cannot be easily associated with the psychology of modern women. For better or worse, women have gained a consciousness that is characterized by the history of patriarchal culture. This is precisely the awareness that today enables women to begin to ask their own questions of the world, such as how they can connect their daily lives with the spiritual sphere. In so doing, of course, she runs the same risk as man, that of separating herself too much from the instinctive ground of the unconscious, of rejecting her "primitive" part and striving for spiritual perfection.

The second risk is to identify with the matriarchal mentality because of the strong fascination with the archetype of the Great Mother. This can be seen, for example, in the preoccupation of many women with the 'witch,' whose modern myth-making has little historical significance. K. Sejr Jensen's "Trolddom i Danmark" (Witchcraft in Denmark) clearly indicates that those accused of witchcraft were elderly or old women from the lowest social strata of society. They were victims, but they were not martyrs of an early female consciousness. This applies to the Danish material.

There are none of the juicy, erotic cases that flourished at our southern neighbors, which, although they do suggest a collective projection of elements previously associated with the religious rites of the great goddesses, must be seen as a collective attempt to suppress matriarchal psychology in favor of patriarchal psychology. But it was a cultural issue, a collective psychotic epidemic on par with the mass killings of Nazism, and it affected victims indiscriminately. When I say that in recent years, a strong fascination has been emanating from the archetype of the Great Mother – so far with quite different results from those mentioned above – it certainly has an effect on male psychology as well. If this were not the case, I do not believe – without underestimating the efforts of women – that the women's movement would have been so successful. Men are not only influenced by women but also by the fact that their own hitherto unconscious femininity has a much greater influence on them than before. There seems to be a pronounced psychological difference between men of the older and younger generation.

To my mind, the big question is how to bring eros and spirit together. For the woman to contribute to a solution to this problem, she cannot "just" deal with the spiritual part of the animus. She must connect with the distinctively feminine principle of the spirit, which in its highest form known to us is expressed in the figure of Sophia. Sophia means wisdom, and we still have her in the word "Philosophia" philosophy, which means love of wisdom. How many male philosophers would agree that the heart should be part of their quest for wisdom? Most equate heart with brain and wisdom with intellectual truth.

My wish for the future is that at least some women will consider it a task to work for "Philosophia" in the true sense of the word, a task which, realistically speaking, is for the few but which is of paramount importance for the many.

Chapter 3

Animus Development in the Individuation Process

Dream Series

Now, I have already described the development of animus at a mainly theoretical level. This may be all very well, but many people will probably ask themselves, well, what is actually going on? How do you do it? There are really only individual answers to these questions. If a woman wants to transform her animus, there is no other way than to give herself to a transformative process. Of course, such a development can take place, as it were, of its own accord in the face of life's tasks. In an analytical process, one tries to speed up the process by bringing in the products of the unconscious and confronting consciousness with them. But it is not enough to understand the messages of dreams intellectually; one must put them into practice. Since this is both painful and difficult, not all analyses can be said to follow an individuational course.

Expectations are also often more modest: The analysand feels bad and wants to feel better. If the process is to go further than that, there must be pressure from within that is stronger than the ego and its inertia, and which drives the development forward. But the ego must also be strong enough to endure the inner tensions; otherwise, there will be no transformation.

So, what I can do to show how a transformation occurs is to give an individual example of it, concentrating here on the dreams that have to do with the animus. These are picked out of a larger set of dreams, but they will follow in chronological order. In this dream series, as in the one in the chapter "The individuation of the female", I will show in practice how to work with dream interpretation based on Jung's theories. With regard to the theoretical prerequisites, I must refer the reader to Jung's works.

The dreamer was a woman in her mid-20s. She had a pronounced animus problem, which manifested itself in part through her attachment to a rather dysfunctional husband, onto whom, of course, she projected her own unrealized potential. She felt that he was a kind of 'mis-recognised genius' and that she had to help him find himself. Meanwhile, her own – as it turned out –

creative abilities lay fallow. You could say she was living below her level.

This is, of course, in a way, a good starting point for an analysis because it means that there are actually quite a lot of positive forces to release. A person who starts analyzing in a self-overestimating state will find for a long time that the analysis robs her of all the fantastic gusts of air that she is actually finding so difficult to let go of. Her difficulties are just a kind of biting that she just needs to get sorted out in order to fly straight up in the air!

A little way into the analysis, the woman dreams:

> *An excrescence has grown on one of my thighs, it looks exactly like two full-grown strawberries placed on top of each other. I walk around and ask several people if they know what it is, but nobody knows. Someone cuts off a splinter to examine it. It does not hurt, but it bleeds. At first, I was horrified by the growth, but then I realized that I had to do something about it myself. Then I grab the root and yank. The whole excrescence breaks off; it is plant-like, with roots sticking out and embedded in the leg. I realize that it comes from some small green burrs that attach themselves to the skin and push their hooks in and grow and turn red.*

This excrescence, stuck in the thigh, undoubtedly represents the woman's animus obsession – it is distinctly phallic. It is loose now that she simply grasps it firmly and pulls. That same night, she also dreams:

> *I am a teacher, and I used to be a substitute teacher. A girl who was little then has grown up. I think it speaks for itself. There has been a psychological growth.*

Another dream follows the same night:

> *It's something like a kind of scouting test; I'm crawling around in a strange landscape with strange paths; everything has to be done in a certain way to be right, but I think I'll make it.*

This dream marks the beginning of a process of individuation. The psychic energy that has been released by uprooting the "excrescence" is now made available for psychological development – the soul journey, if you will.

The very next night, the travel motif is developed. The preliminary goal and task of the journey becomes clear. She dreams:

I arrive in a remote old-fashioned town where I was supposed to meet my boyfriend, but I don't find him and get lost. Then I meet a young man, whom I recognise from the place where I first arrived. He has red hair. He lights up so much at the sight of me that I can't help but smile. He immediately joins me, telling me that he had never dared hope to see me again, but now he will not leave me unless I insist. He will help me find my boyfriend whenever I want him to because he is well-known everywhere here. He says that he loved me dearly from the moment he laid eyes on me, but he will never force himself on me. He then becomes my companion around the country – always thoughtful, loving, and full of good ideas. At some point, we are pursued, maybe by some soldiers, but he comes up with all sorts of tricks, and we shake them off. We never find my boyfriend. Then suddenly, we are walking in a delightful forest. "Where are we going now?" I ask. "I want to show you something," he says secretively. We come to a sort of farm, a very lovely place. There are servants bustling about, hardly concealing their delight that a lady has apparently come to the farm at last. I embrace him and invite him to sleep with me. He is lovely and has been so good – I want to please him, even if I don't love him. Then I realize I have a tampon in my vagina and want to remove it, but I wake up.

Here, we see that the unconscious sets up a contradiction between the dreamer's boyfriend and the archetypal animus. The fact that she thinks she has to find her boyfriend but never actually finds him suggests that the animus projection she has on him is not grounded in reality. What is important is the encounter with the archetypal animus. He appears here in his wholly positive function as a "soul guide" in the inner world. He is "well known everywhere

here," as the saying goes. The red hair emphasizes his archetypal character. From ancient times, red hair has characterized the 'solar hero,' associated at once with the element of fire as passion and love and with the sun as spiritual light. It may seem like a lot of emphasis to place on the perhaps random appearance of this animus – but wait and see! We shall meet him again. This is my advantage in the presentation of this development – I know the whole dream series and, therefore, know before the reader what will prove essential. Practically speaking, if such an archetypal motif appears early in analysis, one should, of course, be cautious in interpreting it, but it should not escape one's attention.

The archetypal characteristics of this animus are also represented by the fact that he is master of the unconscious, master of the lovely estate in the forest. At the same time, the woman's problem is made clear: She doesn't love him, her willingness for sexual union may be fuelled by positive feelings, but this is obviously not enough. She has a tampon in her vagina, which must first be removed. It represents a barrier in her own emotional preparedness that cannot be removed as easily as a tampon!

Viewed *ultimately,* that is, from the point of view of optimum development, it could also be said that this union, if it had taken place here in the forest, would have been premature. It would have put the dreamer in a situation like that of the heroine in fairy tales, the climax of which is her abduction by the prince. It would certainly enable her to find a more suitable boyfriend than the one she had, but this would be done by projection and would not lead to the integration of inner values.

A small interlude in the dream hints at the nature of the problems that lie ahead for the dreamer. These are the soldiers who pursue the couple and are tricked by the cunning of the animus. These represent a collective masculinity that plays a role in the outer world as much as in the inner. A woman may reject the soldier mentality of society, but somewhere in her own psyche, it is a reality to which she is unconsciously connected. Here, the dreamer runs away from the problem – but it comes back. Seen in the light of the different phases of the woman's development, it is a question of the *captivity in patriarchy*. This is not just a personal problem for a woman but a collective one.

Here, I touch on something that is usually difficult to understand, namely, how Jung's theory of the collective unconscious relates to the actual reality we live in. Every person is consciously or unconsciously a carrier of the problems of his or her time, and a process of individuation involves finding a way in which a person can personally live in the field of tension between subjective fulfillment and the socially shared reality. If the collective problems are not realized in a very personal way, the only way to find a solution is through projection. That is to say, by adopting some form of collectively characterized *ideology*.

In the dreamer's case, she evidently had a totally inadequate, not to say naïve, attitude to this kind of problem. Sometime after the dream referred to, when many things have been going on in the mind, it reappears again with full force:

I've been invited to a sort of weekend camp with revolutionary aims. I've probably imagined something like a cozy, working weekend with a bit of teaching. But I'll get a lot wiser. The work is actually not the main thing, but it is an education in a revolutionary ideology that I find myself completely left out of. I try to reason with them, but the more I try, the more unpleasant they become. Some of the guys are downright brutal to me – it only gets really bad after I refuse to sleep with one of them. It's not accepted; you can't put bourgeois ideology into sexual intercourse. I say that it's not for me, I want to go home – but I can't do that, that would be treason. Then it gets worse and worse; I am humiliated, e.g., one of them forces me to dive into a mud hole; it's a big red-haired guy; he sees how it disgusts me and therefore becomes even more humiliating in his behavior, then he spits in my face. I sniff it up by accident.

I have always been very afraid and have almost tried to hide a little along the way. But now I get angry despite my fear; I think that I have always talked about human dignity, and yet my own is almost destroyed now. I tell the redhead that I would like to work, but he won't give me a chance to, even though that's supposed to be the main point of this place. It seems that it actually pacifies him; I am left in peace.

Now, I know a girl who is in the camp and has a high status there; she is married to the leader, who is a skillful and dynamic leader and ideologue. I think I met this girl somewhere else, and it's her fault that I got there. She is a beautiful, somewhat Madonna-like-looking girl, very warm and gentle. She has seen how I am suffering, but there was nothing she could do. But now she comes and whispers that I'd better get going while the leader is away from the camp, and she shows me how to write down the meals I've had on seashells that are gathered in a bracelet I'm wearing. Then she stamps on top as a receipt. Apparently, this is to serve as a sort of pass for the guards outside the camp. I just need to get to the road; then, I can easily get back to town.

The naïve attitude towards left-wing revolutionary ideology is evident in the dream. "A nice working weekend and some teaching!" The dreamer was politically unaffiliated with any party but had a slightly unconsidered sympathy for the left. In real life, she had never experienced a situation even remotely similar to the one in the dream. This is a collective problem. It has long been pointed out by the women's movement how little room there is for women's values in these "revolutionary ideologies." It has been said that the role of women has been "to make tea for the revolution." The captivity of women in patriarchy is not, psychologically speaking, the exclusive preserve of traditional bourgeois/Christian society! Although, in theory, the left has reacted to Christianity's hostility to the nature of humans, it is clear to see how easily it falls into the same ditch and becomes puritanical and hostile to eros, now on ideological-political rather than religious grounds.

The dreamer is thus unconsciously caught in a contemporary conflict that she cannot escape from simply by trying to behave sensibly. She tries to reason with them, and this trait reveals how easily a woman is caught up in such a web. Through her animus, she overestimates the power of reason and imagines that she can "talk her way out of it." Things get really crazy when she refuses to accept the typically male view of sexuality as something that should not be subject to "bourgeois ideology." Surely, as mates, we should be able to help each other out with a bit of an outlet for the instincts! Not a few animus-orientated women have bought into this, not least because women, too, suffer from having been brought up with a prudish and puritanical attitude to sexuality. The average male's idea of liberation is more along the lines of having sex with anyone who wants to. For a woman, it has to be an eros situation if she is not to feel hurt and abused afterward. You can meet many women who seem to accept one-night stands on male terms – but ask them how often they secretly wait for a phone call afterward anyway.

The worst of all the men in the camp is a red-headed chap. I hinted that we should meet him again. How can we understand this figure as an expression of the animus-solar hero, as negative as he is? Well, in this version, he must be understood as the shadow side of the male solar principle in the form of the rigid and brutal soldier mentality. All archetypal images have two sides, one positive and one negative. The degree of development of consciousness can be measured, among other things, by the ability to face the negative side – and transform it. The positive side is more like a gift that is given to you – or so you think. There is always a bill to pay.

In this dream, we see that it is precisely the encounter with humiliation that makes her mobilize all her strength. This happens when the redhead spits on her. The spit, like other separations from the body, has a magical meaning. Like male semen, it is perceived as fertilizing and creative. For example, in his autobiography, Jung recounts how, in Africa, he noticed a religious rite that the natives performed every morning at sunrise: They spat in their hands and then turned their palms up towards the rising sun. It was not the sun itself that they worshipped but this highly numinous moment when the forces of darkness give way to light. In the ancient Egyptian creation myths, the creation of humankind takes place when the creator god masturbates or spits on the mud to bring forth life. When the redhead spits on the dreamer, she finds herself in a mud hole. Mud is also considered a fertile element. It is the unformed but potentially fertile part of Mother Earth. On a completely archaic, symbolic level, there is, in fact, a union of something very primitive, male and female, in the psyche. This is the turning point of the dream itself, which also makes it clear that the motif is not an expression of a female masochistic attitude.

The next subject is the beautiful, Madonna-like girl married to the camp leader. She apparently represents all the traditionally feminine qualities that are otherwise lacking in the labor camp – she is gentle and warm. It is only at this point that she is able to step in to actively help and show the dreamer a way out of the camp. The pass is a bracelet made of mussel shells on which the meals are signed. The mussel is an ancient symbol of the female gender: Botticelli, for example, depicted his foam-born Venus standing in a mussel shell. Furthermore, it is hardly a coincidence that it is the meals that are to be acknowledged, as traditionally, women have been responsible for feeding the family – and in a broader sense, the Great Mother also symbolizes everything that is nourishing for body and soul.

But her friend's position is highly ambiguous. She belongs in the camp. She has literally married power. The camp's leader seems to personalize collective ideals of leadership: He is skilled, dynamic, and ideologically sound. In other words, this figure is the bearer of the collective norm of what to think and how to think. This juxtaposition of the marriage of the very feminine and the very masculine in the unconscious means, of course, that the dreamer still has a long way to go in terms of her female identity. It is a shadow-animus marriage at the archetypal level. As yet, it is beyond the dreamer's abilities to dissolve it, but we shall come back to that.

A few very important dreams follow in a very short space of time before the theme resumes.

I am lying in a room in my bed under the window. A violent storm is raging outside. Even though we are only at its edge, further away, it has hurricane force. Later, I walk out into the storm and see the roofs of houses shaking and lifting. People are worried about the damage it could do. But somehow, I am not afraid of the storm.

The storm is an archetypal symbol of the male spirit. Wind is called pneuma in ancient Greek and also means breath and spirit. In the Christian creation myth, God blows his breath into man to give him life. The power of the wind in this dream says something about how strongly the male principle is activated. People are even worried about the damage it could do – you could be blown away, for example – but the dreamer is not afraid. We may assume that she has actually gained something very fundamental in the previous dream so that she can now experience the male in all its overwhelming power without losing her footing. On the inner level, the dreamer is brought back to that psychological phase which we called the invasion of the *patriarchal uroboros*.

In the various dreams, we have thus been systematically led backward from the encounter with the man for which she was not ready, through the female's imprisonment in patriarchy, and now back to the primal manifestation of the male in the female psyche. That this journey back is not a regression but a necessary part of the individuation process is shown by the following dream two nights later.

After a lot of trouble, I arrive at a large open space with a pole in the center.

Here, we meet the first manifestation of the Self. This is frequently found in simple geometric overall pictures and appears as a center in the unconscious, compensating for the fragmentation of consciousness. The large open space symbolizes the female element, and the pole the male. We find a similar kind of symbolism in Indian Tantric imagery, where the union of the female and male world principles is represented by the lingam in the yoni. This is a stylized version of the sexual and creative union of the God Shiva with the goddess Shakti. In the imagination of this mythology, sexuality was not perceived as separate from the spirit; the union must truly show at once the physical-sexual union and the supreme spiritual fusion of two divine principles.

After this dream, there is very little dream activity for the next ten days, but then there is another big dream that seems to lead to an actual solution to the problem of the animus sun hero:

I come to a strange place; I know a girl there, she is exciting, Madonna-like (this is the same girl as in the previous dream). The place is by a kind of castle, like at the foot of it, into a cliff. Behind the house, there is a big garden. The girl says that she was once intimate friends with the king, but nobody knew it. But the son of the steward of the castle (this is their house) did not socialize with the king, even though he lived there. The girl says that this illustrates the difference in this place. Then there is something about her boyfriend, Bo, in his hands, which must be interpreted to mean that he will die in a 1½ year's time. But time is very strange here because it's as if it has already happened once. Bo comes, and I see his hands; I know he's going to die, and I'm a little afraid of someone I see death in. There is also something rough, woodenly stiffened about his face, a mask-like expression. But he has the most marvelous deep red hair.

In the garden where we are, there are terraces towards the far end, and at the back, there is a small pond and a red thing with a telephone, which has the special ability to call through time and space.

There is also a little girl of a couple of years old and an elderly lady. I play with the child while Bo and the girl, the loving couple, are cooing in the garden. Now, time is so compressed here that the 1½ years is the same as 1½ days, and then he dies. I see him lying by the pond on his stomach, motionless.

But now, a mystery is about to happen. Because it has already happened once, many years ago, that he died, he has now come back to die and resurrect for his beloved.

He is lying there by the pond alone. But as I look at him, he starts to move. I'm scared at first because it might be something monstrous showing itself. But instead, he is transformed. The woody mask from before has disappeared, and the lines in his hands have also changed. Now he is saved from death.

I immediately tell the girl. But she is now strangely semi-interested, although he, who was her great love, has come back to life.

I'm standing up by the house, and I have this beautiful child in my arms; she has the most marvelous red hair. The elderly lady suddenly says. "Now you can see who is mother and daughter." There is no doubt that she means me.

Bo hears it; he is just coming towards us – alone. I know from the color of his hair that he is the little girl's father. He says to me: "Would you like to have a child with me?" I whisper shyly, like a schoolgirl: "I would because you have such lovely hair." I have loved him from the moment he woke up by the pond and have thought of the girl that she did not appreciate him enough. But it's strange because it's as if we've already had a child together, the little girl.

I run down to the red phone in the garden and call myself out into the real world to my boyfriend, who is asleep. I've been gone a lot longer than I thought. He won't understand, even if I explain what has happened. I go over to wake him up.

This is indeed a very long and complicated dream, but every detail is important, so I must ask the readers to try to keep their attention. The scene of the dream is clearly in the unconscious – outside normal time and space. Past, present, and future are linked in the strangest way. It is myth-time, it is the 'once upon a time' of fairy tales, it is the 'dreamtime' of which the Australian aborigines speak in their myths. Furthermore, it is a place very close to the archetype of the Self. The King's Castle, located on the top of the rock, again represents the union of the male and female elements, for the rock or mountain is the place of the Great Mother. Like the medieval castles that were placed high on the cliff tops, it constitutes a protected fortress while at the same time being the center of the whole landscape, including the psychic landscape. Medieval castles were built as mandalas, just as mandalas are often drawn as fortified castles.

In this dream, it is quite clear that the 'friend' is an archetypal figure, an incarnation of the eternal feminine. In the previous dream, she was married to the chief ideologue; in this dream, she has been close friends with the king, that is, with the representative of the masculine Self. But, she cryptically tells us that the son of the manager, whose house we are in, has had no dealings with the king, and this is supposed to illustrate the difference in the place.

How are we to understand this strange motif? I believe that the castle manager and his son must represent the masculine collective psyche, which ideally should uphold the highest male principles. This is a collective-psychic phenomenon because it tells us that the son, i.e., the contemporary guardian of male values, has lost almost any direct connection to the numinous values that underlie patriarchal society. He just looks after the castle. Such a situation could lead to a rigid attitude towards something that is no longer a living value in the psyche. This is a picture of what the situation in our culture looks like.

But now the girl is waiting for her beloved, whose name is Bo. The dreamer knew no one by that name, so we must understand it symbolically as *bo*, which in Danish means dwelling place, nest, or home. Again, we meet the animus with the red hair. But his mimicry is characterized by a wooden, mask-like quality. This again points to the rigid attitude. Now, it is a psychological truth that when an attitude is taken to the extreme, it becomes rigid, and it is at that very point that an opposite movement can set in. The attitude can then turn unmediated into its opposite, or a transformation can take place. A true transformation will very often take the form of death and rebirth. That is what is to happen to the solar hero animus here. It is said directly: A mystery must happen!

Most people in our culture have lost any connection with what a mystery really is. For many, it rather corresponds to the plot of a crime novel. But in ancient times, and in so-called "primitive" religions, the mystery was still alive, and people could draw psychic nourishment from the mysteries that were ritually celebrated. In fact, we also have such a ritual in the Christian Church, namely communion, where the flesh and blood of Jesus is symbolically transformed into spiritual nourishment for the faithful when they drink the wine and eat the wafer. In Denmark, there are probably not many people anymore who experience any mystery about it; the ritual decays and becomes a mere external form.

We have ancient myths that detail the death and rebirth of the sun hero or sun god. In ancient Egypt, the sun god was called Re or Amon-Re. He was a cosmic god, primordial god, and creator god, and was therefore also the lord of all life and order in the human world. Every morning, he rises in the eastern sky, and every evening, he goes to rest in the west. At night, he sails through the underworld, through the realm of the dead. Every evening, he dies, and every morning, he is reborn. The rituals of mankind guarantee that he can maintain his dominion, and his personal representative on earth is the Pharaoh. Pharaoh, the king, is Re's son. Re incarnates in each new Pharaoh, and each dead Pharaoh is transformed again into the sun god. This happens concretely through the process of embalming. The archetypal motif in the dream becomes clearer as we are told that the event has happened before. Insofar as these things can play out deep in the collective unconscious, they are subject to eternal repetition. They are eternal patterns that repeat themselves, as birth, life, and death do at the most elementary human level. What is important for human consciousness is to enter into a real relationship with what the mythical themes represent. For the solar hero to become a psychic life-giving factor, a mutual influence between the conscious and the unconscious must take place. The result must be put into practice, into real life. Otherwise, the images sink back into the unconscious, where one must once again wait for them to approach consciousness.

There is always a "psychologically right moment." If you are inattentive at the crucial moment, you can lose it all again. It is like in fairy tales, where the sunken city rises to the surface once every hundred years – you simply have to be there to see it and to take something home with you. When the human pharaoh died and was reborn, he became a god. Here, it is the reverse process – an archetypal heroic figure is humanized. This explains why the girl in the palace loses interest in him. She is also an archetypal figure, and her love affair with him prevents the dreamer's ego from coming into contact with this animus. But through his transformation, he enters into contact with the human world, and there is a separation of the archetypal pair of eternal male and eternal female.

The little red-haired girl now turns out, quite unexpectedly for the dreamer herself, to be a fruit of this connection. She is an image of the "divine child," the new personality, the fruit of the encounter between the conscious and the unconscious. She is the beginning of a true Self-realisation. It is an "older woman" who makes the dreamer aware that she is the mother of the child. She represents the "wise old woman," a counterpart to the wise old man. Her domain is, first and foremost, the secrets of nature, including the world of female instinct and the whole biological cycle from young girl to mother to old woman. The scene takes place in her domain, in a lovely garden, which I have already referred to as feminine.

In his transformation, the animus of the solar hero has lost its rigid 'wooden' character, and his function as an erotic figure becomes clear. This was the major problem in the previous dream, where the dreamer was trapped in an emotionally cold, masculine world. At the same time, we can also see how the whole process of transformation has profoundly affected the dreamer's own attitude. The reader will remember the first red-haired animus, the master of the farm in the forest – she could not yet love him. But the moment the transformation takes place – she loves him.

The end of the dream may seem a little strange, but she re-enters the ordinary world and finds her boyfriend asleep, thinking that he will never understand where she has been. But it simply refers to her personal situation at the time of the dream. She had long since given up her original relationship and had fallen in love with another man. He was a foreigner, and she herself was very doubtful that it was something that could develop into something more. Not long after the dream, she realized that this distant infatuation dissolved into thin air; one might even be tempted to think that she had projected her animus onto him, who was so conveniently far away so that her inner processes could proceed undisturbed reality.

This is, of course, something that happens very easily whenever the animus of a development is constellated: It is projected onto a partner. When a woman is in the middle of a developmental process, it is imperative that she carefully separates what really belongs to her partner and what belongs to herself. This is, of course, extremely difficult and sometimes painful because the feelings are there and cannot simply be analyzed away; they have to be lived through in the deepest seriousness.

When dreams of this type occur, they often contain something future in relation to actual reality. Although the divine child is conceived and born in the soul, the animus figure nevertheless speaks in the future: It points to something to come. In the dream, the time is given as 1½ years. It seemed to fit very well. In fact, that is how long it took before she was able to realize in real life some of the possibilities that had come to the surface. This involved an independent creative endeavor. At the same time, she also met a man with whom she was able to have a completely different kind of equal and intense love affair than she had ever known before. Three dreams from this later period illustrate this:

Long train journey. At a point where we have got off and are walking on a path along some bushes, I spot a butterfly. It's big, beautiful and distinctive. It's very rare, we take it with us. We have to be careful not to hurt it.

The butterfly is a symbol of the soul; one could briefly interpret it to mean that the dreamer has finally brought the soul in its entirety with him on his journey. It is rare – as all souls are rare, just as all people are completely individual – if they can bring their whole selves with them. It is also something to be handled with care and attention – otherwise, the wealth can be lost again.

Another dream refers more to the creative activity.

I have a golden, cylindrical container. Someone or something has entered it from outer space. Later, I'm on a big stage, and I have to present them, who now seem to be human-sized.

The golden container is the female Self. The contents of the collective unconscious have entered it, so to speak, have entered consciousness in such a form that something can also be given out again for the benefit of other people. The wealth can now be utilized in the stage of life itself. And finally:

It's like a kind of novel. The man and the woman – who is also me and my boyfriend – met once in a forest. There were many complications, but now they are finally together in a close embrace, filled with deep love. The woman says to the man: "I promise you never again to divide my femininity into reason and emotion."

Chapter 4

The Woman and the Feminine

A Female Typology: Mothers and Daughters

In a way, it is easier to talk about the development of women in relation to men than it is to talk about the development of women in relation to the feminine.

Firstly, we are used to thinking in terms of opposites. If you cannot agree on anything else, you can probably agree that masculine-feminine is a pair of opposites.

Secondly, the masculine is more visible and more well-defined than the feminine. Because we live in a male-dominated culture, the words we tend to use for the masculine are clearer and more positively charged than those we tend to use for the feminine. We can also express it in the sense that the feminine, as such, is more unconscious.

Paradoxically, this also means that modern women, in a rejection of the old female gender roles, can easily feel compelled to turn away from femininity in general. One of the prominent women in the women's movement, Suzanne Giese, says in an interview in Alt for Damerne [a women's magazine]: "Many of us early feminists let ourselves down by putting aside our own femininity and sexuality to try to assume a stronger position both in society and in relation to men. We castrated ourselves in a way, but the result of such an attitude is that it becomes impossible to find out how to have a proper relationship with both oneself and men." "I had the backward thought in me that it was impossible to be respected on an equal footing with men if I was a sexual object. That's why I hid my femininity. "I didn't believe that the two things could be reconciled. This was partly because the femininity I had come to know through my mother was useless to me." I think Suzanne Giese is expressing a generational problem. A lot of modern women have not been able to identify with the femininity they have come to know through their mothers. It seems that one of the fundamental differences between women and men is reflected in their basic relationship patterns. Girls and women aim for identification, boys and men for confrontation.

Now, if the first basic psychological identification of the daughter with the mother fails, we speak of a negative mother complex. Psychologists of all schools of thought have long attributed psychological disorders to the "bad mother." And of course, there are "bad mothers" in the true sense, but there are many more mothers who have been as good mothers as they could be. When a whole generation of women complain about their bad mothers and are filled with strong negative feelings towards them, anger, disappointment, contempt, and resentment, I do not think the cause is due to the individual mothers alone. Of course, it has often been said that the mothers' generation has been victims of the external conditions of society that they had to accept. But I think there is a deeper, archetypal influence at work.

At the beginning (see above) I mentioned that the first wave of women's liberation at the turn of the century sank back into the unconscious in the 1940s and 1950s when women, in general, tried to identify with traditional gender roles. If we look at our culture as dominated by the father archetype for many centuries, it becomes obvious that the mother archetype has been pushed into the unconscious. Only very limited forms of expression of the feminine were allowed: The beautiful, the good, the pious, and the pure. All other expressions were suppressed or "demonized." Not only by men but also by women themselves.

It is now common knowledge that if a hitherto unconscious or repressed content of the psyche is about to make its way into consciousness, its first manifestations are often chaotic and accompanied by strong and often negative emotions. What is true for the individual is also true for the culture in this context. In so far as the mother archetype is arguably emerging in our world from centuries of repression, it is no wonder that the Great Mother is angry and bitter. By this, I mean that a good deal of modern women's anger against their mothers is, in fact, not only directed at them as persons but is rooted in the archetypal background of the feminine. Anger is bottomless until it can be brought into an archetypal context, into a common feminine pattern. When the archetypal woman behind all women, through the transformation of the individual woman, achieves the complete expression she demands, the anger is extinguished, and reconciliation with the personal mother can take place.

In the above, I have tried to show that the development of the woman's animus must go through an entirely personal approach to both the collective social norms on the one hand and the archetypal images on the other. In the same way, a development and differentiation of the feminine in the woman must take place. This can be at least as difficult and require great courage of spirit. No preconceived ideas about what women are or should be will help here.

And yet – for me, there are some basic principles. If the development of the animus in the woman aims at introducing objectivity, discernment, clarity, and rationality into the woman's consciousness, the development of the feminine in the woman aims at developing her capacity for relationships, to experience meaningful connections, to sense the organic growth of things and people, to be physically and psychologically connected with the rhythms of life. And, of course, not least, to give women a fundamental feminine identity. But how this feminine identity expresses itself in concrete terms, through which channels, and in what ways – and how much weight the masculine aspects have in her personality – depends on the woman's actual aptitudes and characteristics.

A Feminine Typology

In his book "Psychological Typology," Jung, in part, described his well-known division into introverted and extraverted types of attitude and, in part, his less well-known division into the four types of function. He believed that consciousness constituted a kind of compass, where it could make logical judgments through the thinking function, value judgments through the feeling function, perceive what is actually present (what can be perceived by the senses) through sensation, and orientate itself through intuition to the possibilities that lie behind what is perceived.

The development of consciousness, which begins in childhood, leads to the differentiation and development of one or two functions, which become the main function and the *auxiliary function*. The functions of consciousness are organized in two pairs of opposites: thinking and feeling in relation to each other and intuition and sensation in relation to each other. If, for example, thinking is the best-developed function, intuition or sensation will be relatively easy to make conscious and combine with the main function. For a scientific researcher, it will often be a case of thinking and perceiving combined into a theoretical-practical approach, while the more speculative, philosophical-minded will often have intuition as a second function.

The feeling function will, however, pose a major problem for this type; the person who lives with the head will find it difficult to listen to what comes from the heart – not least because what comes up is so primitive and sentimental that the distance to the conscious attitude is simply too great. It is very easy to identify the thinking type with a man and the feeling type with a woman, which Jung does to a certain extent. This difference is probably largely culturally and environmentally determined.

One might wonder whether Jung's typology is at all as valuable for feminine psychology as it is for masculine psychology. Toni Wolff has posed this question in her article"[7], Structural Forms of the Feminine Psyche. Wolff writes p. 269, "The man's problems are different, insofar as being more dualistic by nature (co-coordinative or formative abilities and instinctively), his cultural achievements are determined by the spirit. Consequently, his conscious attitude and his way of coping with reality are usually based upon the most differentiated function. A woman, on the other hand, is by nature

---

[7] In: Studies on C.G. Jung's psychology.

conditioned by the soul, and she is more consistent in that her spirit and her sexuality are colored by the psyche. Thus, her consciousness is more comprehensive but less defined. The psychic element tends to manifest itself in such forms of life as may correspond to the female structural form and to the cultural period concerned. Not every period offers optimal possibilities for this, but we cannot here go into all those historical, sociological, economic, and religious causes which nowadays hamper the realization of the structural form inherent in a woman."

Wolff believes she has established that there are four feminine structural forms in the female psyche. She calls them Mother (and wife), Hetaira, Amazon, and Mediator ("medial"). They have in common with Jung's psychological types that they are arranged in two intersecting axes and that one or two of the forms are usually predominant in the female psyche, while the third and fourth can only be consciously integrated in the course of life and with great difficulty. Since all four forms can be identified in cultural history, they are archetypal structures.

What distinguishes Jung's typology from Wolff's structural forms, then, is that Jung looks exclusively at the orientation of consciousness, whereas Wolff emphasizes different kinds of relational modes. I consider this valuable because it emphasizes the psychological background to the various female gender roles such as mother, wife, daughter, and mistress, all of which require a relationship with others. Even in the "objective" roles in society, it is clear that women place more emphasis on personal relationships, community, and groups than men do.

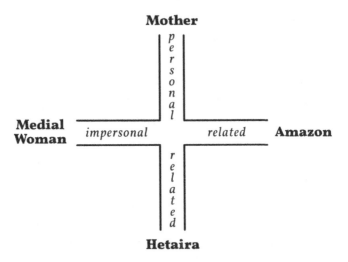

Furthermore, I consider it very important that these structural forms can be used to drive a stake through such clichéd statements about women as: "all women can only be happy if they become mothers" – or the opposite, currently more fashionable, statement that the desire for motherhood in women is an illusion created by society and that, on the contrary, women can only be happy by realizing themselves, unbound by men and children.

In reality, there would probably be about a quarter of all women who would subscribe unconditionally to the former and a somewhat larger group who would be fully in favor of the latter. The first quarter would probably be the mother types, while the second group would consist mainly of Amazonian and medial types. The hetaira types would be somewhat in between because they could imagine a life without children but hardly without a man. The Amazon type is more likely to toy with the idea of having children but no husband. The mediator type is perhaps the easiest of all to disappear into thin air.

It is obvious to some extent to associate the mother type with the sense function, the hetaira type with the feeling function, the Amazon type with the thinking function, and the mediator with the intuition function. However, since the structures outlined are archetypal, it is not possible to link them unequivocally. Rather, Wolff's "typology" represents a female pattern that can help the individual woman to understand which basic psychological pattern primarily characterizes her life. It can also help women to realize that there are other women whose paths and values are different from their own but who can nevertheless contribute to the expansion and expression of the feminine universe. Here, I will give my own version of the four types

The Mother Type

Of all women, this type will be the one who supports and nurtures all that is weak and undeveloped. She may possess an almost boundless selflessness and self-sacrifice. For her, it is a great fulfillment to have children and see them grow up under her loving care. The positive version of this type is, in short, identical to the very ideal of womanhood in our post-Reformation society. She is also praised when she takes on motherly duties in a more figurative sense, like a Florence Nightingale or a Mother Theresa. She is usually based in the home. Her husband is more of a "father" and "provider" to her, and she is the classic wife type who is really quite uninterested in understanding her husband as a person. We are also familiar with the negative version of this 'good mum', as other expressions of femininity have become permissible. So, we get the image of the familiar overprotective and possessive mother who cannot let go of what she nurtures, cannot allow her children to grow up and break free, and cannot understand that her husband's needs in his development will eventually be different from the need for maternal support in his career. Thus, for her, too, the ideal of motherhood can become a neuroticizing factor in the course of her development. She has to learn to do something for herself, too, and she has to learn to say no to all those who need her all the time. This is difficult for her, but if she does not, she will easily develop martyr tendencies, a well-known feminine form of protest.

The Hetaira Type

Hetaira in Ancient Greek means 'female companion' or 'companion'. In ancient Greece, a hetaira may have been a prostitute, but she was often highly educated and respected. In our society, she often takes on the role of a mistress, perhaps as a muse or 'la femme inspiration' as the French call it. You could say that she is the typical "father's daughter." In our society, there are two apparently very different versions of this basic pattern. One we could call the anima woman. This is the woman for whom men's reactions to her are of paramount importance. She has learned early on, through her father's anima, how to act in order to capture his interest, and she carries this on into her relationships with men. She stages herself for a performance on the stage of life through careful dressing, make-up, etc. It is these women who feel like nothing if they do not have a man to mirror themselves in. But through her talent for mirroring, she simultaneously provokes her partner's anima development. The emotional connection between the two is at the center of her interest, and thus, she runs the risk of perpetually becoming the "understanding lover." What she needs in the course of her development is not least to discover her very own feelings – and learn to take them seriously, even when they contradict her husband's expectations of her. As the mother type is bound by collective expectations, this type is bound by personal ones. Both must necessarily develop their awareness of themselves and their own limits in order to reach psychological maturity.

The second hetaira version takes more the shape of Athena, who sprang from the forehead of her father Zeus. It is the comradely side of her that is more predominant than the erotic side. She is the wise daughter who mirrors the intellect and spirit of men. She will typically be her partner's co-worker and assistant, but she will have difficulty going into areas that did not first spring from his head. The courage to bring her very own thoughts into the world can be a milestone in her development, for it is very difficult for her to separate her achievements from the love she expects for them. Of course, this is not without reason either. Many modern men are attracted to this type, where cooperation, love, and companionship can go hand in hand – but woe to her if she suddenly threatens his intellectual position!

The Amazon Type

Wolff has also taken this name from antiquity. The Amazons were a female society, a female warrior people led by a queen. They only liaised with men to breed children, and even then, according to the myth, they only kept the girl children. In our Christian culture, this type of woman has not had much scope for fulfillment until recently. Many feminists belong to the Amazonian type, as well as many career women. They are women who develop a strong and often very competent ego, and their achievements should in no way be seen in the light of any man. Their love of knowledge, intellect, and work stems from their own subjective needs. Autonomy and independence are keywords for the Amazon type. She is basically a "mother's daughter," and behind her stands the virgin archetype: the woman who does not "belong" to any man. In a positive sense, she rests in herself, but in a negative sense, she is characterized by an emotional inaccessibility that can make it very difficult for her to enter into a deep love relationship. It is precisely in relationships with men that the warrior woman emerges. She fights against the tyrants among all men, and one of her developmental tasks is to realize that the tyrant is not least in herself as a negative animus.

She runs a high risk, like men, of identifying with her brain-ego alone and thus perhaps getting caught up in her own ambitions. Many Amazonian types instinctively seek to compensate for this by seeking the company of other women.

Historically, the Amazon type in our country is related to the saga women of the Viking Age. Strong, skillful women who could wield a sword if they had to. One might get the impression that the Amazon type is more common in the Nordic Region than in other countries. Women's equality with men also came to us earlier than in many other places.

But for some centuries, cultural norms have prevented the positive expression of the Amazon type – and so we still seem to be struggling with its distorted image: The cool, distant, passive, "Nordic" type of woman. She is somehow trapped in her own inner world. Like a Sleeping Beauty, she attracts many attempts at conquest, and her worshippers may well get caught in her thorns. On the surface, she does not seem combative, perhaps never expressing a definite "no" and seemingly living up to collective expectations, but she is not there. In analytical practice, one can encounter this type of mother behind a man's anima problem. I would say that this is also the problem reflected in Hans Christian Andersen's fairy tale "The Snow Queen." Eigil Nyborg[8] interprets the Snow Queen as the negative version of the Great Mother and notes that it seems unsatisfactory in the fairy tale that a transformation of this figure does not take place. "The Snow Queen still sits in the mirror of reason as an uninvolved observer of life, whose glow she dims with her icy coldness." To a question about Hans Christian Andersen, Marie Louise von Franz[9] replied that she thought he was very neurotic, but that his neurosis was also the problem of the whole of Scandinavia, namely "an enormous sex problem caused by an apparently Christian prudishness with a very wild, pagan temperament underneath."

Today, there are many examples of Amazonian-type women whose puritanism is emotional rather than sexual. Ice cream by day and hot coals by night! But because they avoid emotionally committed relationships, they actually remain virgins, no matter how many men they have known.

---

[8] The inner line in Hans Christian Andersen's fairy tales, p. 153.
[9] Interpretation of Fairy tales, p. 152.

The Mediatrix

Wolff calls it the *medial* structure. By this, she says (p. 278), one should not think of parapsychology, although the ordinary, spiritualist medium represents the lower, unconscious stage of the type. What the mediator type is linked to is, above all, the collective unconscious. She intuitively picks up what is in the air and seeks to transmit it in some form.

Often, these are impressions of what is in the environment but of which she is not conscious. If she now uncritically brings these things up, plays them out, or expresses them, the result can be very damaging, both to those around her and to herself. She cannot distinguish between her own and others' but is flooded with unconscious content. The boundaries between the Self and the unconscious are easily blurred because her psyche is porous internally.

If she can develop a firm ego and differentiated discernment, however, it is a different matter. Then, her consciousness can begin to relate to the impressions she receives from the unconscious – and then she can begin to function in earnest as a mediator. In our culture, the type has had very few opportunities for positive and recognized expression. A few exceptions have been the great religious female talents – and they had to recognize a nun's existence. In ancient and primitive cultures, the mediator type has had its place as seeress, sibyl, oracle priestess, and shaman. They have all been women whose task was to discover what was still in its infancy – to uncover the will of the 'gods', something that concerned the whole of society. Today, the mediator type can be found in the irrational "professions" – such as an astrologer, graphologist, chiromancer, tarot reader, healer, etc. Among the modern "witches" in parts of the women's movement, there are probably not so few of the mediator type, and in my opinion, there are also many of them who completely miss the point by simply identifying with the constellation in the collective unconscious. Such identification is detrimental to personal development. One identifies with something that is not one's own, that is bigger than the Self, and that concerns the culture as well as the individual. The lack of conscious integration also easily leads to an uncritical acceptance of even the most primitive nonsense and rubbish at face value, e.g., indulging in black magic, which is nothing more than an ordinary lust for power in an exotic disguise.

For the mediator type, it is as important as for the other types to become aware of her own very personal psychology, its strengths, and weaknesses – only then can she begin to relate in a genuinely mediating way to the contents that are constellated in time. Wolff writes[10]: "The objective and collective psychic contents, however, can only be adequately expressed in an objective language which, apart from art, would have to be a psychological or symbolic one."

I suspect that among female analytical psychologists, there are a number of mediator types – myself included. When I was very young, I also tried my hand at artistic expression to give form and language to what I sensed. I was drawn to and fascinated by all those places where the irrational and the mysterious thrived. I gradually realized that in me, inner and outer somehow coincided, so time and again, I had to realize that what I "happened" to be interested in "happened" to appear soon afterward as a current in time. But only after I began to analyze and learn the language of dreams could I begin to separate myself from the collective projections. I learned to sound an inner alarm bell when I started to get "caught up" in something so that I could dampen my own enthusiasm a little. I learned to use other functions of consciousness to make distinctions – and that this was highly necessary because not everything that one senses or is gripped by as a mediator type is something that should be brought out.

Thus, although each woman must first and foremost become aware of her own primary psychological structure, all four types are present in all of us, and a process of individuation involves becoming

---

[10] Studies on C.G. Jung's psychology p. 281.

aware of them. Through our maternal part, we relate to our biological, nurturing, and nourishing part and the psychological functions that have been differentiated over millennia from the instinctive root. Through our hetaira part, we relate to the opposite sex; through our amazon part, we relate to the ego and its capacity for independent activity; and through our mediator part, we relate to the larger psyche in which all human beings share and which carries within itself the seeds of the future. No part can be missing if it is the wholeness we *seek*.

Mothers and Daughters

Every woman is a daughter. For every woman, the first love is directed towards the mother. How this first connection subsequently manifests itself in the woman's psyche depends, therefore, not only on the personal mother but also on which part of the feminine structural forms is most prominent. Together, these four forms a kind of overall picture or compass of the feminine. Depending on the starting point of a woman's psychological development, what is fairly easy for one woman becomes very difficult for another. But whichever path a woman takes, it inevitably leads to the question of the daughter's true emancipation from her mother, for only then can she gain an independent identity.

Unconsciously identifying with one archetype or another keeps women stuck in certain patterns, which in our culture have been patriarchal in nature. The modern woman is not content to play the role of the well-behaved daughter or the good mother. Here, despite the pioneering work of the women's movement, we are still standing on partially virgin territory. It is not enough to do away with the external forms of gender roles if they still bind us internally.

Colette Dowling writes in "The Cinderella Complex," p. 177: "A woman without a useful role model faces a serious psychological dilemma. She does not want to be "like a mother." Nor does she want to be "like a father." So, who should she be "like"?"

To answer like the cat, "I am my own damn self," does not really work either. A woman is part of a deeper, more comprehensive pattern, and she must learn to recognize her place in it, but at the same time, in her individuality, to be a unique combination of that pattern. Deep down, mother and daughter are one. They have never in our history been really separated from each other. Jung writes[II]: "The psyche which exists prior to consciousness (e.g., in a child) shares in the maternal psyche on the one hand, while on the other hand, it reaches over to the daughter psyche. We could, therefore, say that every mother contains her daughter within herself and that every woman extends backward in her mother and forwards in her daughter."

My three-year-old daughter seems to express the same idea when she talks about wombs. She is very interested in the fact that she has been in my womb, and I have been in my mother's womb, "and," she says, "when I grow up, you will be in my womb, and I will give birth to you." She is, in fact, expressing the age-old idea of cyclical return, which was dominant, e.g., in the old agrarian societies. Here, the woman's sexuality was considered sacred because it was of the same nature as the creative power of Mother Earth, and through her biological cycle, the woman formed a parallel to the great cycle of nature, the germination, growth, and death of the grain, the changing of the seasons. Sexuality was sacred because it was the expression of the fertility of all things.

Jung's article that I quoted above deals with the Demeter myth (in Homer's Hymns). Demeter is the Greek goddess of fertility, and Kore is her daughter, who is abducted by Hades, the god of the underworld. The myth is mainly concerned with Demeter's anger and the attempt to reconcile her. The daughter Kore is completely passive and 'flower-like.' Jung writes on p. 219: "The figure of Kore, which interests us here, belongs, when observed in a man, to the anima type, and when observed in a woman to the superior personality type ... The figure corresponding to Kore in a woman is

---

[II] Introduction to Essays on a Science of Mythology, p. 225.

usually dual, i.e., a mother and a young girl, which means that she sometimes appears as one, sometimes as the other." Jung thus recognizes that it is the same archetypal figure that is anima in the man and "Kore" in the woman.

Furthermore, Jung states (par. 311): "The maiden who crops up in the case stories differs not inconsiderably from the vaguely flower-like Kore in that the modern figure is more sharply delineated and not nearly as "unconscious." He also notes that Kore appears in women's dreams and fantasies as an unknown young girl, as a dancer, as a maenad and nymph. The girl's helplessness exposes her to all kinds of dangers, such as being eaten by reptiles or sacrificed. There may also be a descent into the realm of the dead and a search for "the elusive treasure," sometimes also associated with orgiastic sexual rites or, for example, sacrifices of menstrual blood to the moon. Behind all these rites is a 'mother earth' figure.

Jung goes on to write (par. 355) that "these maidens are always doomed to die because their exclusive domination of the feminine psyche hinders the process of individuation, that is, the maturation of personality. The "maiden" corresponds to the anima of the man and makes use of it to gain her natural ends, in which illusions play the greatest role imaginable. But as long as a woman is content to be a femme à homme, she has no feminine individuality. She is empty and merely glittering – a welcomed vessel for masculine projections. Woman as a personality, however, is a very different thing: Here, illusion no longer works. So, when the question of personality arises, which is, as a rule, the painful fact of the second half of life, the childish form of the Self disappears too."

The woman Jung depicts here is the man's woman – the woman who is identified with patriarchal norms of what it means to be a woman. She is too much daughter and too little in touch with the Mother Earth part of the female psyche. I would call the Kore figure the daughter archetype when it comes to women's psychology (anima in male psychology). The childlike, helpless form of the daughter archetype must, therefore, die in order for the woman to become a personality. The daughter archetype represents the transforming part of the feminine. It is the daughter who transforms, not the mother.[12]

In 'The Golden Ass,' Marie Louise von Franz comments on the Amor and Psyche myth. On page 75, she says that Psyche can be considered a variant of Kore (in the story, she is considered an incarnation of the goddess Venus). "We have to ask first what the difference is between the mother and daughter goddess, and in general, we can say, looked at mutatis mutandis, that the daughter goddess is closer to the human than the mother goddess, just as God the Father is more removed from man than Christ. The same nuance is true with regard to Kore. The girl goddess is closer to humanity, a more incarnated form of the mother goddess, and Psyche would be a still more humanized form of the Great Mother Goddess. She is in a form which has nearly reached a completely human level, and only her name says that she is still a goddess."

What does it mean that the Mother Goddess "incarnates" herself? We are not talking here about something theological but about something psychological. It is about the fact that the archetype, from being projected out into the world as a deity out there, is instead given its humanized, individual expression. "The 'gods' move into the psyche. They disappear from the world. Nietzsche famously even declared that God was dead. For some time, our culture believed that religion would disappear more and more and be completely replaced by a rational, scientific view of life. In recent years, we can observe that this is not the case. *Homo religious,* the religious human being, cannot be replaced by *homo faber,* the technical human being. When Jung's ideas about archetypes and the collective unconscious were declared mystical and religious for many years, it was meant in a patronizing way at the time, but I think that today it is precisely Jung's respect for the religious and

[12] Cf. Neumann's distinction between the elemental and the transformative aspects of the female in: The Great Mother, p. 28ff.

mystical side of human beings that is helping to increase interest in his work.

Looking at the events of the present from the perspective of mythical events allows a different kind of interpretation of the world. It allows us to look at the psyche 'from the outside,' so to speak, in a different and more meaningful way than that which merely describes human behavior in statistical terms.

There are, of course, societal factors that have created the opportunity for women's changing conditions in this society. I do not want to deny it or underestimate it, but I would argue that it is not the whole story. Behind collective social movements are collective movements of the psyche. Events happen simultaneously outside and inside. Women (and men) who are part of these events act, think, feel, rejoice, and suffer. There is an inner force as well as an outer one.

Today, when the woman stands there as an adult, independent, responsible person and seems to have gotten what she asked for, she may realize that along the way, the meaning of it all was lost. She has lost the connection with her roots, she has cut the umbilical cord to the endless chain of wombs that have bound her to the primordial mother from the beginning of time.

Then, the daughter's search for her mother begins. In the ancient myth of Demeter and Kore, it was the mother who sought the runaway daughter. In modern women's literature, it is the daughter who seeks the mother. Sometimes, this search finds expression in the so-called women's utopias, where the mother is found in a comprehensive, supra-personal version of a highly developed matriarchy. Utopian societies are created where the Great Mother reigns, and her daughters can live.

We can also observe this search back to the mother in some actual female endeavors – matriarchal collectives, goddess movements, and lesbianism by choice.

The problem with many of these endeavors is that they also exclude all male values. In the mother-daughter unit, there is no room for men. However, since men are half the world – to use an inverted feminist slogan – I do not believe in these endeavors as a solution for the majority of women. They are in the nature of psychological regression – an escape back to the mother, back to the first stage of a woman's psychological development, the stage of self-conservation.

It is psychologically naive to believe that the Great Mother represents all good and the Great Father all evil. The sorting between good and evil is something we do with our consciousness, with the ethics we have as individuals, or at least according to the norms of a group. The Great Mother is both dark and light. She kills with one hand, gives birth, and nurtures with the other. It is hard to imagine that old Mother Earth was in moral conflict with herself when she sent floods or droughts to one person and gentle rainfall to another. Her "wrath" is as great as her "love".

In this part, we have, in fact, a parallel in most of the "old" gods, including the Old Testament Yahweh. Mercy and blessing alternate with punishment and wrath. Women today cannot remain standing in their outrage at oppression. With equality comes equal responsibility. However, being equal and responsible is not something that is enshrined in legal clauses. It must be experienced as a reality by the individual.

If I have been a little critical of certain modern female experiments, I must at the same time say that I believe they also have a positive character – because a return to the origins is also a new beginning. Other women whose path is less extreme can also find inspiration and renewal in this. Their main task will be to pave the way for a synthesis that can respect the values of both men and women. I do not know how all this might shape up in the longer term. I feel that all these currents are still in their infancy. For it is the task of an age, hardly the task of one or two generations. But I know that very important things are stirring deep in the unconscious. An elderly friend of mine told me a dream that made the deepest impression on me.

She had visited a Buddhist temple on a trip to Sri Lanka. A young native pulled her along to show her around – for a tip, of course. In the end, he insisted on showing her the statue of the future Buddha, and she was so annoyed that she spontaneously exclaimed: "How do you know that the future Buddha is not a woman!" He was appalled, a woman! That was unthinkable! But shortly afterward, she had a dream:

> I saw a very large, slightly dark-skinned, primitive woman coming towards me. In her hands, the woman carried a dark blue velvet cushion. On the cushion was a little naked girl, one or two years old. I realized that she was still too small to be away from her mother. When the big woman came very close to me, a voice said: "This is the future savior of the world."

It is a dream so crystal clear and numinous that it is hard to imagine it having "only" personal meaning. Indeed, my friend felt it was a gift – something that did not belong to her alone. Here, we have an image of the female Self on an almost cosmic scale. And it is represented as mother and daughter. The primitive woman undoubtedly corresponds to the nature side, the "Mother Earth" part of the feminine. She is the mother, the Great Mother, who has recently given birth to a daughter. And this daughter is directly referred to as the future savior of the world. She is still too young to be away from her mother, i.e., she cannot yet function as an independent psychic entity. To determine her nature, we are given a single key in the dream: She is sitting on a deep blue velvet cushion. My friend said that it was the kind of thing that could be used, e.g., to carry crown regalia, i.e., something that emphasizes a very valuable symbol of the central power. But it is not a king's power, but a queen's power, since it is a girl. The blue color is associated with heaven and with the activity of the spirit. The Virgin Mary also wears a blue cloak. This little girl is, therefore, associated with the spiritual aspect of the feminine, with the Queen of Heaven.

I think this is something very central. Modern women cannot "settle" for the archetypal image of the ancient mother that underpins her biological existence as a woman. She needs consciousness – and she needs spirit. The dream thus seems to point to the fact that the daughter archetype is reborn as a spiritual being. And yet, she is shown as an ordinary girl. This means that the feminine archetypal transformative activity of the archetype also manifests itself spiritually in the psyche of the modern woman. This corresponds to experiences I have had, which I shall endeavor to show in the dream series in the next chapter, where it is seen that the daughter archetype seems to guide the female individuation process. The daughter archetype shares the Great Mother and the female Self on the one hand and the female ego on the other. This gives her a kind of shadow character for the ego, but she is more comprehensive or 'enigmatic' than shadow figures usually are. The daughter archetype can be activated in this way in women who consciously do not identify with the daughter role but have distanced themselves from it. This can happen in the first half of life as well as in the second. The Great Mother goddesses of old were both nature goddesses and queens of heaven. In our Christian culture, Mary retained only the traits of the Queen of Heaven.

Jung discusses the problem of Mary in "Answers to Job's Questions" and says that the dogma of Mary's immaculate conception and her preservation of perpetual virginity while having the effect of elevating Mary's personality by bringing it closer to the perfection of Christ, was at the same time detrimental to the imperfection, or rather the completeness, of the feminine principle. "The more the feminine ideal is bent in the direction of the masculine, the more the woman loses her power to compensate for the male striving for perfection, and a typically masculine, ideal state arises which, as we shall see, is threatened with an enantiodromia [counter-movement]. No path leads beyond perfection into the future – there is only a turning back, a collapse of the ideal, which could easily have been avoided by paying attention to the feminine ideal of completeness. Yahweh's perfectionism is carried over from the Old Testament into the New, and despite all the recognition and glorification of the feminine principle, this never prevailed against patriarchal supremacy. We have not, therefore, by any means heard the last of it" (par.627)

Jung was very concerned with the Catholic Church's dogma that Mary had been admitted with her body into heaven and had entered the heavenly bridal chamber where, as the bride, she was united with the bridegroom (Christ). It may sound strange that Jung took these things so seriously since he was not a Catholic, but he saw them psychologically. He believed that the development of the dogma gave expression to eternal, archetypal events that had always been "in heaven" but which only became realized when they found their expression in time and space on earth as actual historical events. Jung's interpretation of this dogma was that it must mean that a 'divine child' was now being conceived.

Jung also emphasized the fact that the dogma meant that Mary had been given an – almost – equality with the Trinity, that the male "threeness" had been completed into a "fourness," which for Jung was an image of wholeness. Could we not go a step further and dare to think that the natural "fourness" consists of father, son, mother, and daughter? Our Danish Grundtvig prophesied in his old age that God's daughter would be born – in Denmark! Now, one must be careful not to take prophets too literally, and I do not see my friend's dream as a literal prophecy about an actual woman who will be "the future savior of the world." Such things must be seen symbolically and psychologically as a statement that the spiritual renewal of our culture must come through the female. It seems to me that the very secular beginning started with the burgeoning process of female emancipation about a hundred years ago, in Grundtvig's time.

In my friend's dream, there was no hint of Mary-like purity and perfection. The little savior of the world is an ordinary girl, a paradox that seems to contain a possible synthesis between nature and spirit. There is a material basis for the spirit, and the spirit is born of mater-ia (mater = mother). I said before that I do not think this is the task of a single generation. As you know, we are entering what astrologers call the age of the Water Bearer. We usually think of the water *man*. The symbol holds the possibility of humanizing the 'divine' content. In our context, it is interesting to note that in the Major Arcana of the Tarot cards, the Water Bearer is symbolized by the card "the star" - and is a woman. In "Jung and Tarot," Sallie Nichols writes about this card: "In the psychology of a man, such a feminine figure represents his anima or unconscious feminine side. In a woman's journey, this figure, being of the same sex, would symbolize a shadow aspect of the personality. Since the Star Woman is drawn on a grand scale, larger than life, she could personify a quality far beyond the personal shadow and more akin to the Self, that all-encompassing archetype, which is the central star of our psychic constellation. In either case, the kneeling figure represents a hitherto inaccessible aspect of the psyche, which, like a fairy-tale princess, was formerly imprisoned in a tower and held captive by the cruel King Logos, the ruler of our masculine-orientated society." (p. 301)

But let us come back to the present. When I reviewed the four parental constellations under the section on animus, all of which provoked the daughter's animus development in different ways, there was one common feature: The feminine was weak in all of them. All four patterns create little basis in the daughter for a secure and differentiated female identity. There is no balance between the male and the female; there is a predominance of masculinity, whether it comes from the mother's animus or from the father's ego and shadow. This corresponds to the undifferentiated expression of the feminine throughout our society. The feminine "strengths" are amputated into a form usable by the male and, therefore, do not become equal.

We are also accustomed to considering animus alone as an expression of the spiritual in women. Earlier, I mentioned that I do not believe that the spiritual side of the animus can be integrated if there is no corresponding development of the feminine in the woman. Then, the spiritual animus has the effect, which Jung also mentioned, that the feminine expression becomes perfectionistic and strives for purity, and thus places itself a little "below" the masculine spiritual ideal.

Now, I believe that in this constrained situation of the feminine – both in women and men – the daughter archetype emerges in the psyche as the expression of a feminine spiritual activity, which is not, however, separated from its instinctive foundation. In the process of individuation, then, we must set as an optimal goal that the woman, on the one hand, is brought into contact with the Great Mother and the instinctive part of her own psyche and thus can free herself from her own mother, but also that, on the other hand, through the activity of the daughter archetype, she is connected with the transforming aspect of the feminine. This is a future-oriented activity. This is the *puella aeterna* archetype – not as the eternal daughter in relation to the spiritual values of the fathers, but in its archetypal activity as the beginning of the new. Through the transforming activity of the daughter archetype, a woman can enter as an equal partner in the renewal of the cultural and spiritual values that are so urgently needed. It is this very need that has called her forth from the psyches of women and men.

Chapter 5

Female Individuation

Of course, individuation is something – individual. The female soul journey, its death and rebirth, and its encounter with the Self are something that the individual woman must experience in order to realize her uniqueness as a woman. Male individuation, after all, has some fairly well-described phases: The hero's separation from the world, the integration of the shadow, his search for the elusive treasure, the night journey through the unconscious, the defeat of the 'dragon' and the conquest of the anima – and finally the realization of the Self, or rebirth. Death and rebirth play a huge role, mythologically and psychologically, with rebirth corresponding to the synthesis of the conscious and the unconscious. As Jolande Jacobi puts it in "The Way of Individuation," p. 89, "it involves an attitude that can best be adopted by one who knows from personal experience to what degree the part is always obligated to the whole (society, the collective) and yet remains a whole in itself."

The big problem when you look at most of the material, the myths, the alchemical phases, etc., is that it is almost always seen from the point of view of male psychology. We cannot simply assume that the female individuation pattern is identical to the male. Since consciousness in our long culture has been male-dominated, the known myths, etc., will, to a large extent, compensate for and expand the male consciousness. In this sense, the land of the unconscious is more clearly mapped out for the male psyche. But the woman has historically held the place of the unconscious. Myths that refer to the female unconscious, the matriarchal psyche, are archaic and alien, showing patterns that may seem strange or even repulsive to many a modern female consciousness. However, this distance in time is compensated for by the fact that the woman's ego is often less rigidly rational than the male ego, and she nevertheless gives herself up more easily in the process. But could we find some phases of female individuation? While I was wrestling with this question, I came across an article that seemed to be just what I needed.

In "Surfacing and the Rebirth Journey," Annis Pratt outlines a series of phases that she has found to be typical of a large number of British and American women's books of the type that, in a more or less symbolic way, send a heroine on a search for her own identity. She emphasizes that the heroine's soul journey seems to be somewhat different from the heroes. What is interesting to me is that her findings also seem to cover the spontaneous material produced through dreams, so much so that I have been able to use her phases as headings for the dream series we will be looking at shortly.

Pratt writes that she understands the female ego or persona as that which lives in an everyday world of cultural experience, which is, by definition, a world of family and social norms. This same mode of being, in my formulation, is also reflected in the unconscious material.

Pratt then sets out a schema of seven phases, with the reasonable reservation that not all phases are, of course, present in all novels. (p. 139ff) I will largely omit her references to women's fiction since, in this context, it is the actual phases of individuation that interest me.

Phase I. Separation from the Ego World.

This first phase starts with a sudden realization of dissatisfaction with the typical roles and norms in which the heroine is trapped. This realization leads her to take the leap into the unknown, so to speak; she starts her inner journey into the matriarchal psyche.

Phase II. The Green World's Guide or Sign Helps the Heroine Across the Threshold.

Here, the heroine is helped across the threshold of the unconscious by an apparently ordinary phenomenon that assumes an extraordinary significance. This phenomenon belongs to the natural world and may come from an animal or a natural phenomenon. In our dream series, as in Atwood's book 'Up to the Surface,' a lake becomes the entrance.

Phase III. The Confrontation with the Parental Figures.

This is not a confrontation with the parents at the level of reality; in the novels, e.g., this may be made clear by the fact that the parents are dead. It is about an inner encounter with the parents that reaches down to the parental archetypes deep in the unconscious. This encounter is key to the journey ahead; the parental images must be transformed in order for them to function as archetypal guides. In our dream series, particular emphasis is placed on the mother image and the way it changes – from being an obstacle to being a helper.

Phase IV. The Lover in the Green World.

This animus figure is distinctly non-patriarchal. The encounter with it is primarily concerned with the heroine's initiation and the integration of her sexual and natural energies, the inner Pan (an ancient nature deity). It may be as an ideal, super-personal figure, a deity representing fertility and death and rebirth, it may be an animal, e.g., a buffalo or a unicorn, or it may be that a human lover in this phase takes on superhuman dimensions on a fantasy level. In our dream series, this lover is represented by the male Moon.

Phase V. The Shadow.

This phase involves a struggle with and an acceptance of one's worst sides, one's anti-ego. To avoid terminological misunderstandings, I must emphasize that in Jung's psychology, the shadow always refers to a person of the same sex as oneself. But Pratt's "shadow" is male. So, I would call it an animus figure. It is very negative and can be symbolized by a "devil" or by demonic, life-denying, and self-hating characteristics. Interestingly, Pratt says that this "shadow" stands for power and death in the matriarchal world. This is consistent with my experience that the shadow, in the Jungian sense, does not play nearly as big a role for women as it does for men. But this is the case with this demonic animus, which we shall also encounter in our dream series and which I also consider to belong to the matriarchal layer of the psyche.

Phase VI. The Final Descent to the Nadir.

In this phase, the heroine is taken to the deepest places; it is a dangerous phase that, in fiction, can lead to madness as well as to transformation. A chaos of surreal images and symbols appears. They represent the actual experience of death, where the heroine either disintegrates or experiences the point of transformation in her quest. But even if the heroine is able to make the leap through this layer of being, she will have problems with the ascension phase and her return to normal society. In our dream series, this phase also involved an inner crisis and an "initiation" into the dark, subterranean regions.

Phase VII Ascension and Return to the Known World.

For the fully transformed woman, her return to society is more difficult than for the male hero because, Pratt says, the 'elixir of life' won by her is not only devalued by society but is a threat to it. This is why, she believes, so many of these types of novels end inconclusively. Sometimes, however, the heroine is provided with a 'new space.' Although the heroine is unable to influence the wider world, she is often described as passing on her 'elixir' to a younger woman or initiating herself – as a daughter – in relation to an idealized mother figure. And finally, Pratt says, the transformed heroine seems to pass on her 'elixir,' not to anyone within the text but to the female reader.

These 'solutions,' unsatisfactory in the traditional sense, in my opinion, point to several things. First, a big question mark: What happens when women start to become themselves? It is something new that women are struggling towards such a consciousness.

Secondly, many of these protagonists are driven by their own – contemporary – neurosis, and the self-transformation is primarily a healing process (if successful). It is psychologically very realistic that an influence on the surrounding society does not automatically result from the transformation. The possibility is left to the future – to the younger woman, to the reader, to a utopian matriarchal society. But – and this is even more important – such a transformation is the necessary precondition for an influence to gradually take place. Those who go first always have the fate of not reaping the fruits of what they sow.

Let us now turn to how self-transformation is reflected in the spontaneous products of the unconscious, i.e., in a series of dreams. The dreamer was a young woman with a typical problem of the time: She was rather negative towards all traditional female values, home, children, and husband. She was afraid of becoming seriously attached to anyone, not least because she feared falling into a typical female role of dependency. She was outwardly well-functioning but inwardly shy and undifferentiated in her own femininity, like so many modern women.

She feared too much intimacy while also longing for it. In such a situation, of course, one cannot give oneself fully. No woman can do that unless she has a secure sense of who she is as a woman and as a person. She is then incredibly vulnerable and covers it up with aggression or escape mechanisms. Experience has shown that such problems are associated with unresolved conflicts in the early psychological phases, including in relation to the mother. But in order for the development to be said to have an individuation course, the spiritual energy bound up in the personal conflicts must be converted into a transformation of symbols, which then takes on an archetypal character. It is precisely through this that the process can acquire a general female interest.

Phase I. Separation from the Ego World

Dream: *I go somewhere with my grandmother, who is very old; there is also a sweet "nanny" and another woman, blonde, very beautiful, but peculiar. She tells a story about when she played at the tables in some casino; she behaved in such a way that the men would pay for her, told them stories about her sad fate, and with her beautiful face, she enchanted them so that they ruined themselves for her. She will try that again, she says and sits down outside. We are at a fashionable place.*

Later, I am sitting on an air mattress in a swimming pool with a male friend; we are journalists or detectives or something. There are many people around the pool. I see the blonde girl walk along the edge, look out over the water, and walk on. I look at her face, which has a peculiar expression. – She's going to jump, I say and follow her with my eyes. A little later, she really jumps. I shouted to my friend, but he didn't notice anything, so I had to explain. We dive after her but keep catching a dark, pageboy haircut girl who just looks at us. Finally, we see a shadow under the water and get her, too; she's dead. Nobody is very interested. My friend doesn't care either; he's more interested in the dark girl we fished out. I notice her shirt on a chair; it bears a champion swimming badge. I discreetly take it off her shirt and give it to her without him seeing it.

In the opening scene, the dreamer is traveling with her grandmother, and someone is called a 'nanny.' A curious name for someone who looks after an old lady. And yet, it is significant. Because it implies that the "grandmother's" attitude has aged to the point where it corresponds to that of a small, helpless child, it is at once the end and the beginning. The blonde, beautiful woman corresponds to a shadow side of the dreamer. She is a negative hetaira type, combining the tools of the courtesan with cool calculation and apparent helplessness for the purpose of material gain. She also represented to the dreamer everything that she rejected in her more feminine sisters – she could never do that! But then the shadow revealed itself with the continuation, "and I could never do such a thing either" – there was just that tiny element of annoyance or envy that women who "could never do such a thing" feel towards those who can and do!

In the next phase of the dream, she is sitting in a swimming pool with a male (platonic) friend, and they have an investigative function – journalist/detective. This presumably refers to the 'detective work' of the analysis, where the analysand begins to become aware of what is going on around the psyche. Then, unexpectedly, the blonde shadow commits suicide. Instead, another female figure of a completely different nature appears. There is something mysterious about her; where does she come from? It seems as if she has been in the pool all along and is only now emerging – unconsciously, we might say. There is a very peculiar connection between the dreamer and this dark girl: She does not let her friend realize that she is, in fact, a champion swimmer, and one wonders how many rescues she really needs! This dark girl we shall meet again; she seems to represent the archetype I referred to as the "daughter archetype," and as the dreamer comes to recognize her, she is referred to simply as "my dark friend." However, at this point, the connection between the two is completely unconscious to the dreamer; she perceived the figure as positive but could offer no explanation as to why, in the dream, she set her animus on her without revealing her true nature.

It was only a long, long time later that she was able to trace the personal origin of this friend to a girl who had been the first friend of her life, whom she had known from a very young age until they separated because the family moved when the dreamer was three years old! This girl was just a bit dark and southern in color. But in the dreams, she is always the dreamer's own age. This is also why – as we shall see later – this friend can be the bearer of an archetypal feminine image, for the little child lives in an archetypal world, and the dreamer's deepest problems are constellated here in the phase of self-preservation, where the dominant archetype is the

Great Mother. But the little friend was a "daughter" like herself, and in the dreams, she could, therefore, come to express all the problems of female identity that the dreamer faced, both in a personal and archetypal sense.

But although this first encounter appears to be very unconscious, it has a profound effect on the dreamer's psyche.

Phase II. Signs of the Green World

> Dream: *I come swimming into a lake, apparently artificially created, with flowers along the sides. It is shaped like this:*

> *I swim into the center and lie on my back with my arms spread out like a cross. It feels very satisfying.*

It is a very important dream. Again, she is out in the water element, which here is almost womb-shaped, and she lies down in the center. It is an act of self-surrender – a kind of surrender to the unconscious forces. It is not without effect. Three days later, the following dream appears:

> There is a small Oriental house. It's carved out of ivory. It's marvelous; the walls are like a filigree pattern. It was screwed into something high up, but now it's on the ground. There's also another woman, my old friend whom I haven't seen for a long time. We talk about the strange little house. There's something odd about the size that changes. The house or I get bigger and smaller. "Call the mistress of the house," my friend says. You have to be in the courtyard and call in a polite oriental

style. I do so, and out comes a very small girl, perhaps 10 cm tall, sleepily blinking.

The result of sincerely surrendering to the process in the unconscious brings about a movement deep in the unconscious: The Self awakens. Here, it is seen very literally: It is a little girl who has just woken up. Nevertheless, she is the mistress of the house, it is said. The fact that her house is Oriental is no coincidence. For us Westerners, the Orient represents the opposite, the very different and unknown. Our recent fascination with Eastern philosophies and religions is largely a projection of the unconscious, but largely missing, spiritual values in our own psyche. We naively assume that they have what we lack and that we can then acquire it through them. But if those inner values are to become ours, we must make the journey ourselves. In his autobiography, Jung tells an anecdote about an old man in a caveman community. All his life, this man had been thinking and philosophizing, trying to express what he had come to. Everyone else watched with interest. At last, he found an expression: A circle with a square that satisfied him. All the others saw it and thought, "Aha, so that's how you do it," and then they all drew circles and squares.

The moral, of course, is that no imitation will do. Individuation requires very personal participation in the process, and no system can do it for anyone, however "right" it may be.

Another feature of the dream shows that we are near the power center of the psyche: It is the strange shifting relationship between size. All space and time relationships seem to be relative in the unconscious so that the smallest can equal the largest. Here, it is a tiny little girl who is the mistress of the house – that is, of the psyche. It is no longer the ego that can claim to be the ruler of her house. In a process of individuation, it is the Self that rules in the background. In a certain sense, one must assume that it is the archetype of the Self that is always behind the whole of a person's development, for individuation meant for Jung, who made a person what she was. In the natural human being, the process proceeds entirely unconsciously, but we are no longer 'natural' in this sense, for the 'I' has gained an ever-stronger place in the course of our cultural development. Consciousness has gained strength at the expense of primordial man.

In the first half of life, individuation is normally directed towards adaptation to the external world, the establishment of self-consciousness, and the relationship with the environment. In actual fact, in terms of family, education, etc., and psychologically, in terms of emancipation from parents and the formation of an independent personality. The ego is thus to be seen as the three-dimensional part of the Self, the part of the Self we are conscious of. The second half of life – typically from mid-life (35-40 years of age) – has a different psychological purpose, which is essentially a preparation for death. This involves establishing a psychic connection with the collective elements of the unconscious, with the myths that sustain the culture. In primitive cultures, the old are the wise. This has also traditionally been the case with us. But when the wise fathers have lost their connection with the living wellspring from which all culture springs, wisdom dries up. This is why a process of individuation is directed towards a living, psychological connection with the whole person. This cannot be achieved by dogmas and ideologies, for these always cover only a part of the individual.

It is not possible to maintain too sharp a division between the first and second halves of life. Behind many of the young person's difficulties in adapting, there is a much deeper need for meaning in life, which cannot be satisfied by therapy that focuses only on adaptation. Behind the youth rebellion and the explosion of women's liberation in the 1960s lie powerful collective forces that are still in their infancy. It is not the generation itself, which is now mature, but the archetype of youth rebellion that represents the renewal of the spirit. It is an age that is coming to an end, and these disruptions deep in the unconscious are causing many neuroses in individuals.

It must always be remembered that it is individuals who are the bearers of cultural change, and in such times of upheaval, it takes more than an average consciousness to accept and integrate such changes, to live them individually on the one hand, and to change the social environment on the other. Inadequacy to one side or the other creates neuroses. They have personal causes as well as social ones. But the battlefield is the psyche of the individual. Becoming what you are often means going against a set of accepted norms, even those considered "progressive." For a woman, becoming herself takes her on a journey into 'woman's land' through the matriarchal psyche, and it also means an encounter with the mother complex, as I have already mentioned.

Phase III. The Confrontation with the Parental Figures

> Dream: *We are going on board a ship, my mum and me. There are a lot of people. I think I'm tired, anyway. I rent a cabin for us; it's easy enough, but the others prefer to huddle together. On the way home, I think I really intend to share the others' conditions, but then I enter the women's bathroom, where it is immensely hot and crowded with sweaty women. At least in the cabin, there were sinks. My mum is more prepared to be with the others; they had to do that during the war. But I want to be myself.*

The ship is itself a female symbol, the maternal womb that carries the individual across the sea of the collective unconscious, protecting and containing it. There are many people traveling here, indicating a tremendous activity in the whole psyche. The problem for the dreamer now is how to enter the very basic female community, the women's warm bathing room. This is a rather primitive image of the female. In Muslim cultures, the bathing room is typically the place where women meet; it is characterized by physicality, warmth, and community. The mother, of course, represents the dreamer's natural connection with that community, and she has more of a part in it. But the dreamer wants to be herself. She does not want to enter into this womb state but to find her own individuality. A few days later, she dreams:

Abroad, maybe in Rome. We are going to attend some lectures at the university. They talk about the change in women that has happened – and another one that is to come. There is a man who will be born with special powers. But time is strange; what is already affected by what is to come, as well as the other way around. That is why I can also do some things when I am connected to him. Several things succeed for me, but I do not place much emphasis on it; I have complete confidence in him. But then they come with a black male cat in a cage; it needs to be healed. I start stroking it as I feel I should, but then I get the thought that it wants to piss on me. It makes me uncomfortable, and in a way it fails. But afterward, I talked to the cat and confided in him what had happened. It says that it actually wanted to piss on me.

Rome is a symbol of the Great Mother. Large cities, in general, are feminine symbols, and Rome, in particular, has a position as the "Bride of Christ" because the Pope has his seat here, and the church is understood as feminine in relation to God. Here, we are far from the primordial community of women because it takes place at the university, where they talk about the transformation of women. This must refer to a change of a spiritual nature. It is further emphasized by "the man who is to come, who has special powers." These are evidently of a magical, healing nature since it is a "healing" that the dreamer is to attempt on the cat. An animus of a spiritual nature is evidently to mediate the healing of a masculine instinctive element in the dreamer's psyche. However, it is important to keep in mind that this healing occurs through the transformation of women.

This motif itself is also archetypal. In our real world, it is almost the problem in a nutshell: The masculine has lost its connection with its instinctive roots; therefore, it is sick. The reconnecting element is female in nature. Here, too, the archetypal motif can be seen in the peculiar relativity of time. Past, present, and future influence each other. In relation to female individuation, it is clear that the woman must have her animus with her in her development in order for healing to take place. Now, the attempt fails in a way because the woman is afraid that the cat will piss on her. It is the female fear that something spiritual will be sexualized, or rather become only sexual! This dreamer, like so many women, had a distinct division in her relationship with men into platonic-spiritual connections and sexual-emotional connections. This corresponds to a split in her femininity. We saw how the female bathing community disgusted her while she gladly accepted lectures at the University of Rome.

Even if the cat is not healed this time, something has been achieved. They can talk to each other in confidence. They are not enemies. And the cat confirms her experience: It actually wanted to piss on her. Now, this instinctive animus is under the domination of the Great Mother, so her fear of it is probably due to her animus-emphasized reluctance to connect with the matriarchal mode of experience. Her problem in relation to her feminine side is still far from resolved:

> I'm planning a holiday to Rome, leaving the next day, everything is ready. Then I find out that X is also going to Rome at the same time, and she talks happily about how nice it will be for us to spend time together. At least we won't be staying in the same hotel, I think, so I can go to museums during the day and just spend the evenings with her.

This recurring dream of Rome is the journey into the feminine universe. She would probably have preferred to travel without her shadow, X. This girl was an acquaintance of hers, very emotional and warm but also very helpless and dependent. The dreamer had very ambivalent feelings towards her, appreciated her emotional warmth and openness, but was greatly annoyed by her helplessness, which she found difficult to stand up to. But there is nothing to be done; the shadow has to come along, of course! She also has to deal with those aspects of her own femininity, which are weak and undeveloped, her dark side (they have to be together in the evening), while her stronger daytime side is more concerned with intellectual pursuits. Of course, it must be emphasized that if this had been X's dream about the dreamer, it would be equally certain that her development would have to be strengthened on this side. Dreams are, to a great extent, compensatory for the conscious attitude. Then again, help comes from the unconscious:

> *I am talking to my grandmother (who in real life is long dead). She is wearing long trousers, a red shirt-blouse, and a red scarf tied around her head – even her hair seems to have a reddish tinge. "How smart and youthful you look," I say. Grandma says that she is also better now than she has been for many years. I think that in this outfit, you can still see the remnants of the beautiful figure of her youth.*

In real life, the dreamer's relationship with her grandmother was not 'red' – she did not radiate much grandmotherly warmth but was a domineering, animus-accentuated woman. Gifted, but like so many women of that generation, she had no opportunity to use her abilities constructively. Now, she has changed; this means that the primordial maternal begins to appear in a more attractive form to the dreamer. An eros bond has been created with the mother image. Then comes another long dream, which seems to contain an archetypal problem that all women struggle with:

> *I am in a small, bright, lovely castle. A lot of people I know are gathered there as if there's a party. Then it's evening, everyone is asleep. I look through a door and see the maids going about cleaning up after the day's mess. I notice one dark-colored girl in particular; she is calm and deliberate as she cleans up. There is not the slightest trace of discomfort on her face. Then there are some girls who have taken part in a theater performance. They are in rococo costumes and light-colored wigs, but instead of being beautiful, they have ugly make-up. They don't like it, one of them tells me. But it had a purpose*

in the play, so I say that it's more demanding to have to act, to play a real role, instead of just looking pretty. "It's easy for you (to look pretty)," I add, not wanting to offend them. Only then do I realize how stupid they are because they respond with surprise and flattery? Do you mean it? Yes, that's quite true.

Then some gangsters appear, who, like in a Western film, lie outside the house and shoot at us - the men inside return fire, the bullets drum away, and one after another fall. We women – who are not participating – have to lie down on the floor to avoid being hit. There is nowhere to run because they have us surrounded. Most of the shooting is along the long sides of the house. Then I go to a window in the end wall with another girl – a man comes outside. We shout at him, crying, saying that we women have no part in this, and now we can no longer bear to see the men dying around us. If they will let us out, we will change our protectors. We are still crying and wringing our hands in the style of the last century; we are also wearing old-fashioned, long, dark dresses. 'But,' I say, looking at him bashfully, 'that doesn't mean we can...' 'No, of course not,' he replies quickly and understandingly and hurries away. But of course, we realize that this means we have sold ourselves for freedom. We tell the other women we have no feeling that this is wrong, and neither do the other girls – except one.

I say that it would be good to put an end to these senseless killings. "What is it," this girl now says in a flat voice. I try to explain, but she doesn't seem to understand, and finally, I shout, "Do you want to be killed? "I have no opinion on that; what do you think?" she replies in the same toneless voice. The other girls shake their heads in irritation; they see her as incredibly stupid. But I feel that she is on the verge of a breakdown. Then they stop shooting. "Then maybe we don't have to go with them after all," we say. Then, she realizes the unspoken implications. She shouts: "Fuck, we must sell our fucks for life," and she begins a monotonous rhyme, loud and somber; she shouts: "In and out – in and out." It seems scary to me. I grab her and try to bring her to her senses, thinking that she has had a past that has hurt her, and now she is close to a breakdown – she is my friend. But she says: "Do you want to fuck me, too?" "No, I don't want to; I'm trying to get you out of here alive." She doesn't hear me. "I don't love you," she says. "No, I don't either, but I like you." I take her arm. Then she falls halfway over me. She's taller than me, and I can't actually move, but still, she behaves as if I'm trying to rape her. It looks ghastly – I'm scared – in a moment, she's going to move on to violence. But suddenly, my boyfriend is standing behind her – I see that he has realized the situation, and he will grab her. I calm down.

The dream made a very strong impression on the dreamer, dramatic as it is. In the beginning, the scene is peaceful, and the day's party mess is quietly removed by the maids, among them the dark girl whom the dreamer associated with, the dark pageboy-haired girl who was dragged out of the swimming pool in a previous dream. This is an image of the nocturnal' cleaning function' of the unconscious. Normally, of course, this function is fairly automatic. The psyche must be seen as a largely self-regulating system which, particularly through dreams, 'processes' the ongoing daily events and throws out the rubbish. This corresponds to the normal and indispensable repression mechanism. Small problems during the day are automatically compensated for in dreams so that an excess emotional element is released and disappears. Everyone has 5-6 dreams every night, but only very few people remember all of them. They do not cross the threshold of consciousness.

But the greater the distance between the conscious attitude to some problem and the unconscious attitude, the greater the tension in the psyche. The emotional "charge" will increase, perhaps bringing on a nightmare. When the unconscious images rise to consciousness, they often provoke anxiety. What comes up is what you fear.

Other more positive emotions can also, as we have seen, accompany the dream. There, the relationship of consciousness to the unconscious is more characterized by expectation, joy, and acceptance – as in dreams that provide a solution to a problem, an inspiration, a creative impulse. Here, we are going deeper into the unconscious; there is something that needs to be made conscious.

In the next layer, we meet the dressed-up girls. They are caricatures of a female role – adorable and stupid. They represent everything the dreamer despises about the female; they are collective personas, masks, for the woman. They play on the stage of life, and they play for a male audience. But here, they are wearing hideous makeup "because it has a purpose in the play." In the dream, the purpose seems to be to make them aware of the role they are playing. Vanity is made unattractive, which is very much for the dreamer.

But then the scene changes from peaceful to violent, a battle between the men outside and the men inside! This is the plight of the modern woman: The struggle between the animus on the inner front of the 'house' and the outer male-dominated society. In an attempt to find a solution, the dreamer – and the other women – want to make peace with the men outside by placing themselves under their 'protection.' This is understandable, as the position of women is very weak, but the price is that 'they sell their bodies for freedom.' It is a price that women have been paying for centuries. They have made their bodies available to men in exchange for protection. The female role, that lovely, anima-seducing role that the dreamer has such contempt for, has been the weapon that has given women indirect power over men.

The message that finally gets through to the dreamer is that she herself is playing the game. It is her dream self that wants it and is no longer a shadow figure. She has to take responsibility for this female weakness-female power and realize that it has deeply wounded her own femininity. It will no longer be possible to talk in an intellectual way about female consciousness versus weak, passive women, which is not her problem: Her friend does not want it – she is the only one who resists because she is the one who has suffered psychological damage.

Before she can embrace her femininity in a form other than the traditional one, she must heal her sick friend, i.e., the part of herself that has been damaged.

There are more sophisticated ways to abuse your femininity than by being gentle, passive, helpless, and adorable. The modern, animus-centered woman hurts her femininity by not respecting her own feminine values, e.g., by using her sexuality on masculine terms. By wanting to be the "mistress" of her sexual activities, by replacing puritanism with promiscuity, the woman has simply replaced one set of masculine conditions with another. I have heard a number of women say, almost with pride, that I can have an orgasm with anyone I sleep with (i.e., I am not weak and helpless and bound to a man just because I sleep with him). Where there is no broader erotic harmony, the woman will violate her own femininity with that kind of orgasm. For the neglected femininity, the friend in the dream, it is just a mechanical "in - out, in - out."

The solution to this problem cannot come from any man; only a woman herself can define her own eros and then live it in real relationships with men.

In her individuation process, the woman has to go much deeper into the unconscious to find possible answers to the problem:

I've come to a strange hidden town in the mountains. They don't seem to like strangers because I have to prove my right to be there. I tell them that my mum is from there, but it's true that I haven't been there since I was little. But that's not enough for them. I think I will be killed if I don't have the right to live there. I'm sitting in a room, there are some papers and photographs, I think. I fold them face inwards, and then I have to use some kind of magical power to make the image disappear or change. I don't remember more, but I feel strength within me, and I am sure that I will succeed. This demonstration will somehow provide the proof.

Again, we find ourselves in the magical world of the collective unconscious. It is a city ruled by the Great Mother, enclosed in her mountain and hidden from all strangers. We can directly see the matriarchal trait because the dreamer's mother comes from there. But blood kinship is not enough; she must demonstrate her access to the place herself. The test is a kind of magical transformation process. We are not given any more details, but we can safely guess that it is the transformation itself that is at stake. It is dangerous: Failure means death. Sometime later, there is another dream with the theme of transformations:

> I am working on the dissolution and boiling of some substances. We're in a medieval castle. Others have tried before me but have been horrified by some terrifying creatures that appeared. I'm prepared to take it in my stride, but nothing sinister appears. But the stuff in the pot really does transform into something else. I'm extremely excited and keen to do it.

It is clearly an alchemical process that is going on, the scene is medieval, and it is the dissolving and boiling of some substances in a pot that is going on. Jung demonstrated in several of his books how the medieval alchemical tradition had to be understood as a symbolic, psychic process of transformation in which the unconscious contents were projected into the concrete matter. Here, we see that the psyche's own work is presented as alchemy. Here, the transformation of matter actually takes place in the dream, and the result, which is supposed to be access to the maternal primordial ground, appears soon afterward:

> I've left home, I'm wandering around with my duvet, it's nighttime. I am wandering around looking for a place to sleep, but everywhere they turn me away. I am in "Sønnenborg" [The Castle of the Sons], a very large castle courtyard, where soldiers are seen dimly within the walls and gates – I can't be there. Out in the countryside, I ask a young boy if he knows anyone who can help me. He doesn't.
> I come out in a sort of scrubby area by a river. There, I see some young girls. I remember meeting them before, another time. Then, they wanted nothing to do with me. Even now, they are dismissive at first;

they are very shy, but there is something elfin about them, timeless. "How beautiful you are," I say – and they are, with beautiful heads and high-bosomed bodies. I enter their underground dwelling; they all seemed so young; only now do I realize that some are older, mothers of others. "Will you help me? I need it so much?" I ask. They hesitate. "Then I will help you in return." Then they hand me a brush and a strange hose, I have to clean a wall. It's dirty, but it comes off easily. Suddenly, a relief of a man's head with a beard appears on the wall. Later, I talk to the women. One of the young people tells me that she would like to go to school; she is about 13-14 years old, has never been away from home, and knows nothing about the subjects she has to learn. I want to teach them – they also want to learn. They are ignorant. But they are so whole, so rounded, so free among themselves. There are a few men around, but they are completely inferior in this world of women. It seems to me that one of the older women has been outside – that she is the one who somehow causes the young people to have to learn something.

The dreamer's starting point here is Sønnenborg, an easily understandable image of a masculine world. There are soldiers everywhere. But she cannot stay here, and her animus, the young boy, cannot help her.

Then she comes out into the uncultivated countryside, a scrubland by a river. Such a place, like the city in the mountains, is psychologically dominated by the Great Mother. The ancient great goddesses were also goddesses of wild nature and wild animals. Ancient depictions, e.g., show Inanna or Ishtar standing on a mountain surrounded by wild felines. The dwelling place of the women is underground, in the womb of Mother Earth.

It is this ancient world that Mephistopheles refers to in Faust, Part II[13]:

My power is not sufficient for the heathen,
it has its own hell, you must know;

---

[13] Goethe's Faust p. 348.

however, a remedy is provided".

The tall maple tree, which in the dusk is blurred,
I am only reluctant to reveal. Velan dog - viid:
high Goddesses dwell in the Realm of Desolation,
around them, no space, let alone time;
not easy, it falls, more to say about them.
Mothers are!

Faust:
Mothers! Mothers! - How sweet it feels!

Mephistopheles:
And strange it is. Most distant in the distance,
by you not known, by us not mentioned gladly.
Search deep in the depths of You want something for them;
it's your own fault; we need them.

Faust is, of course, about the development of a man. But the woman, too, must descend into the depths, into the 'heathen world,' into the realm of the mothers. For her, however, since she is herself a woman, it is a question of an encounter with her own psychic ground. The dreamer already has a much more positive relationship with the feminine than before. She has realized that she desperately needs the help of these women if she is to find a permanent place, an identity of her own. And she offers to do something in return. This is a curious feature that is often found in dreams where important things are happening, and it clearly shows that there is an exchange between the conscious and the unconscious.

All these women in the underground dwelling turn out to be mothers and daughters. They are almost indistinguishable from each other. As I have mentioned before, the primordial identity between mother and daughter is a very old feature. The climax of the Eleusinian mysteries centers on the reunion of mother and daughter,

Demeter and Kore. But when Kore returns from the underworld, it is in a transformed form: She has conceived and given birth to a son. Furthermore, her status has also changed: From a girl traveling on earth, she is now elevated to Olympian status: Two-thirds of the year she will spend with Demeter and the other gods on Mount Olympus, while one-third will be spent as the ruler of the underworld, as Persephone, the wife of Hades.

The myth of Demeter shows how matriarchal and patriarchal forms of consciousness clash and yet are connected. From the purely matriarchal point of view, the man is a robber and rapist who abducts the young flower-picking Kore. Female strength is entirely on the mother's side, for she has the power to stop the growth and birth of everything in her anger at the loss of her daughter. This power is recognized and respected by the patriarchal consciousness, and so a compromise is reached. But from a matriarchal point of view, every mother is condemned to lose her daughter to her husband, but she will regain her once the daughter has become a mother herself. Just as the unity between Demeter and Kore is an essential feature, so too is the birth of the son. Neumann writes in "The Great Mother" p. 308: The second element of the mystery is the birth of the son. Here, the woman experiences an authentic miracle that is essential to the orientation of the matriarchate: not only is the female, her image, born of woman, but the male as well. The miracle of the male's containment in the female is expressed at the primitive level by the self-evident subordination of the male to the female: even as lover and husband, he remains her son. But he is also the fecundating phallus, which, on the most spiritual plane, is experienced as the instrument of a transpersonal and suprapersonal male principle. Thus, at the lowest level of the matriarchate, the male offspring remains merely that which is necessary for fertility. But at the mystery level, where the Kore who reappears is not only the Kore she who was raped and vanished but also a Kore transformed in every respect, her childbearing to is transfigured, and the son is a very special son, namely, the luminous son, the "divine child."

This motif is repeated in many variants. Best known to us, of course, is Mary's birth of the divine child Jesus. "This transformation, says Neumann p. 319, presents a typical opposition to the Masculine, whose transfiguration appears as an illumination of the head— solidification, coronation, and halo. True to her feminine nature, Kore becomes a "bearer" of light." The Eleusinian mysteries must be regarded as essentially female initiation mysteries, although they gradually became very popular among men. There was a peculiar male parallel to Demeter-Kore, namely some male mystery initiations whose deities were a male ithyphallic couple, the Kabirs. They appear as a bearded man and a young boy called "Pais." The cult of the Kabirs was, in fact, related to the cult of Demeter-Kore. Kerényi writes in "Hermes" p. 76: "In Thebes, the Great Goddess is named Demeter Cabiria, which betokens her relation to the realm of the dead and also to the Cabiri. In all these manifestations, she is the primordial feminine source of the absolute male principle of the Cabiri, known to us from the myth of the primordial Herma." (Phallus as the source of life and fertility, and spiritually as the male aspect of the source of life.)

Now it is with the two *kabirs* as with the two goddesses: They are identical; at once father and son, the begetter and the begotten, the man and his phallus. The son, pais, is also the son born of Kore. It is with the son aspect that the old matriarchal psyche has its positive relation, not with the mature man.

In this dream, we see a peculiar inversion of the motif: "Sønnenborg," and the young boy, who does not know the way, is up in the world that the dreamer is leaving. The bearded man, on the other hand, is seen to be down in the subterranean dwelling, and it is the latter that apparently needs work. How should we now understand this motif? I believe this is because the relationship between mother and daughter has been reversed: Nowadays, the center of gravity of the transformative activity lies with the daughter. It is now the daughter who seeks the mother in the unconscious. Of course, patriarchal culture has not left the female psyche without a trace. Through its influence, the female ego has become more conscious. The modern woman's consciousness is much more secure than that of her foremothers (and we do not have to go back very far in time). At the same time, however, the old type of woman was in a state closer to nature; the reason why the daughter seeks the mother is that she is seeking her roots, from which the strong development of the ego threatens to cut her off. Here, in the dream, it is made clear: In the unconscious there is an archetypal, unitary femininity to which consciousness has lacked access. But here, there is a lack of consciousness of a structuring element. The woman's desire to 'learn' something corresponds to what the dream ego is doing, namely cleaning the wall where the bearded man's head is located. This symbol must be understood as 'Kabiric,' as an original, non-patriarchal element in the female psyche.

If, in a patriarchal culture, a woman has seen her primary activity in relation to the divine son, leaving the "father side" to the patriarchal definition, it would now seem that it is possible for women to become "self-begetting." According to the dream image, this must be understood in a spiritual sense and not in the archaic, instinctual sense – for it is the man's head that is shown. Just as the mother's psyche relates to the 'son,' so the daughter's psyche relates to the 'father.' But we must expect that there is still a very long way to go for the dreamer in her psychological development before this can be integrated: It is not a living man; it is a relief. It is still underground, in the womb of the unconscious – and the image of the bearded man is very archaic and impersonal. All men have beards. Now, there comes a long period for our dreamer, too, when the feminine is strongly constellated in the psyche; it is the help of the "elf girls." The dreamer is brought to a completely different kind of acceptance of the "primordially maternal" than she has known before; her disgust with the "community of sweating women in the bathroom" disappears.

Something about Christiania has to be moved. But in the end, it seems to be going very well because a big, motherly, authoritative lady has a foot on it.

My mum tells me something about Prinsessegade [Princess Street], before the time of Christiania. She has lived there. She tells about a mum with a little girl who also lived there. There, in Prinsessegade, the little girl was just skin and bones, even though she was a good mum and did everything she could. My mother tells me that she could hear everything that was going on in the flat – when the mother breastfed the baby, she moaned loudly because it seemed erotic to her. Then they moved to Christiania, and the baby became round and happy and very beautiful.

In the dream, we are told that it is a large, motherly lady who is in charge of Christiania; not a big surprise, considering the attitude behind Freetown Christiania's first years. It was to be a place where there was room for everyone, the sick and the marginalized, on a par with the happy and the imaginative, a place where there was a room filled with heart and warmth for all. A utopian idea of matriarchy was central to the early Christians. Very symbolically, the pioneers occupied a super-patriarchal piece of land: Military territory. The mother's story about mother and child in Prin-sessegade may be understood as a story from the unconscious about what did not work between the dreamer and her mother. It was obviously not the mother's personal fault, for she did what she could for the little one – but the mother archetype was not constellated as it should be between mother and child. But in the unconscious, this has now changed – because mother and child move to Christiania, and the child thrives. In other words, the part of the dreamer that has been 'undernourished' begins to take in the compensatory activity of the mother archetype. Prinsessegade is geographically close to Christiania, but there is something symbolic about the name. "The 'princess' is the young, unfinished woman, closer to the daughter than to the mother. This seems to indicate that the dreamer's mother was more characterized by the daughter archetype than the mother archetype. From a family history point of view, this seems very reasonable since the grandmother occupied a very dominant position as the matriarch of the family. We have already seen in a previous dream that the inner image of the grandmother changed character and took on greater warmth (the red clothes). Two nights later, the following dream comes:

> A strange exotic village. It is night time. I am almost alone but accompanied by a man. There was a thick forest that had been cleared and fields to be cultivated. The village is made up of small, strange huts standing on mounds of earth. The man who tells us about it is perhaps a builder or such like. He is very unhappy that the town seems so dead. It does, but I'm sure it's full of life. Little by little, other people are coming; the town is waking up. In a way, the city seems ancient.

This is a nocturnal scene; it is the darkness of the unconscious. The forest has already been cleared, a not-infrequent image of something beginning to become conscious. The fields are being cultivated, and the town is slowly coming to life. The small huts on top of the earth mounds are themselves reminiscent of breasts; it is female nature in a very primordial – ancient – aspect that comes to life in the dreamer's psyche. A month later, she dreams:

> A lot of moving around. But in the middle of it all, I have a baby – a beautiful little baby with lots of hair on his head and big, calm, green eyes. I pick him up a little awkwardly, remembering that you're not supposed to pick up such a small child without supporting its head. But this child can already hold its head by itself. Instead of being a nuisance, the child brings a focus on the confusion – I am very happy about that.

You do not have to work with dreams for very long to come across children as a dream motif. Of course, they can often be interpreted as childlike parts of the dreamer itself, but in this dream, the child clearly has unusual, non-childlike characteristics. Jung writes in "Essays on a Science of Mythology", "One of the essential features of the child motif is its futurity. The child is a potential future. Hence, the occurrence of the child motif in the psychology of the individual signifies, as a rule, an anticipation of future developments, even though at first sight it may seem like a retrospective configuration. Life is a flux, a flow into the future, and not a stoppage or a backwash. It is, therefore, not surprising that so many of the mythological saviors are child-gods. This agrees exactly with our experience of the psychology of the individual, which shows that the "child" paves the way for a future change of personality. In the individuation process, it anticipates the figure that comes from the synthesis of conscious and unconscious elements in the personality. It is, therefore, a symbol that unites the opposites, a mediator, a bringer of healing, that is, one who makes whole. Because it has this meaning, the child motif is capable of the numerous transformations mentioned above: It can be expressed by roundness, the circle or sphere, or else by the quaternity as another form of wholeness. I have called this wholeness that transcends consciousness the Self. The goal of the individuation process is the synthesis of the Self." (par. 278)

We must understand the dream in the sense that it anticipates something in the dreamer's development, which is still in its infancy, but by its anticipation, it already affects the present, as the child 'brings a center to the confusion.' We have already seen several times how dreams directly express the paradoxical fact that the future can change the present and even the past. If this were not possible, how would it be possible to help people through psychotherapy? How else would people be able to transform themselves really deeply and profoundly? The power of the psyche is marvelously great: As soon as we envision a different future, we can let go of our anger and grief about the past to such an extent that the past somehow changes. Our interpretation of reality is so crucial. Some people go through harsh events almost unscathed, while others are broken by something that, to many, may seem quite insignificant.

For our dreamer, the "descent" is by no means over, nor is the confrontation with some very deep-seated – and for the modern woman very typical – problems:

Something about some caves in a fenced area. There is also some water inside the caves, which is unclear to me, but there is a kind of dance going on through the caves and out again; I dance with several men. I particularly like one of them. At one point, another one approaches, and we are sitting outside on a bench; 2-3 other men I danced with before are also there; they protect me from the one who has misunderstood the situation. I say: "I don't want to sleep with any of you." There is a rather cheerful, sympathetic atmosphere. Then my friend arrived. I was glad to see him, but he started to reproach me for my behavior. Apparently, he has been standing somewhere outside and has seen me waltzing in and out. He demonstrates my movements, pointing out something frivolous about them. I shouldn't seem so challenging, he says. I defend myself and say that I have always been very careful about my behavior. But he persists. I realize that he hasn't seen us dancing. "But there was music!" I exclaim. (But it's not without reason that he got jealous because I was interested in one of the men.)

Now, there is an obvious contradiction between what the dream ego experiences – the dancing in and out of the caves – and what her friend has seen. He does not see what she is experiencing. He has seen her moving with other men in a sexually arousing way and is jealous. She, on the other hand, thinks she is completely innocent because "there was music," and she "is always so careful about her behavior." She had completely forgotten that one of the men had become intrusive and that she had to be protected by the others. It can be understood as a fundamental contradiction between a patriarchal form of consciousness and a matriarchal one. The dreamer herself is still rather unconscious of this last form and, therefore, also unconsciously identifies with it while at the same time denying it and arguing with her friend in a rational way.

This problem manifests itself at the symptom level of surrender- anxiety. This problem is one of the greatest for the modern woman. She is torn between emotion and reason, and she cannot find the way to the surrender and devotion that every woman basically longs for. She can rage against her husband, make scenes, or play roles of all kinds, show coldness to be overcome and change to sudden sexual excitement, or, on the contrary, feel loving and gentle and close but then be unable to fulfill it in erotic contact. Or she knows that many things have to be right in order for eroticism to be as it should be and makes enormous and unfulfillable demands on her partner that simply preclude anything from getting started. Or she seeks security in the marital nest and ecstasy in the arms of the "stranger" who will not make emotional demands on her.

She's secretive, and she's capricious, and she is conscious enough to know it and suffer from her changing moods. This problem has its roots deep down in the matriarchal psyche. Unconsciously, the woman has not finished the first psychological phase – the phase of self-conservation – but she has not consciously remained in it. On the contrary, she has rejected it through a strong development of animus. She has developed a strong "head-ego," an animus self characterized by the patriarchal form of consciousness, which thinks clearly and objectively, makes distinctions, and sees facts. And she has completely forgotten her "heart ego." The seat of matriarchal consciousness is the heart because it works with relationships rather than confrontations.

When it comes to the phase of self-surrender in her development, which is supposed to take her beyond the norms of patriarchy and reunite her with her own female nature, she is afraid of it. She is – with good reason – afraid of losing her hard-won clarity of consciousness, afraid of being swallowed up again by the Great Mother. She may be as afraid of the negative, engulfing aspect of the Great Mother as a man is. But this has more fatal consequences for her because she is essentially denying her own nature, her own instincts, and her own spirituality. However, a man can be a man without making the inner encounter with the female. His identity is not threatened. But the woman who denies her femininity and fears the dark caverns of the womb will become more and more animus-obsessed. The warriors of the Great Mother take revenge for the goddess and victimize the woman with explosive outbursts, hateful quarrels, as well as self-destructive depressive periods.

What the dreamer fears is the orgiastic ecstasy; she says: "I don't want to sleep with any of you," and she tries to be "nice" to the patriarchal animus consciousness. The ecstasy is linked to the music and the dancing in and out of the caves, an image of a possible later devotion to the rhythm of the unconscious itself.

The dance is reminiscent of the Dionysian mysteries, where the women (as opposed to the dreamer) entered into orgiastic ecstasy through the music, realizing that they were dancing with the god Dionysus himself.

Inherent in the fear of surrender is the fear of losing one's temper, becoming obsessed, losing control, dissolving, dying, and returning to an archaic state of nature. The journey of discovery into this matriarchal psyche continues:

I am in a faraway country with my friend. The next day we are going on a tour. I wake up early and go out alone, very far away into the desert. I come to a kind of mine; it has some bamboo structures that I have to hang on to in order to move forward. In the dream, it doesn't seem strange at all, but the mine is "upside down"; it's an elevation, an embankment I'm walking on, and these structures, which would normally support the ceiling of a mine, are standing up in the air. It's hard, and I wish I was in better shape. Now, I'm starting to see green land, so I guess I'll be back at the hotel soon. I'm running out of time;

it's getting late in the day. I see a picture of my friend looking angry and nervous. Someone says that he also slept too long. "But why did she just leave," he says. Then, there is a picture of a young dark girl. A voice asks in reporter style, "Why is this young woman on her way to a religious meeting of her community in this strange city?" We see her rushing off in some kind of Salvation Army-like uniform to some building in an exotic city. She looks worried. The voice: "It is not customary to seek out the community of faith – why is this woman doing so?" Now, she enters a room for a kind of prayer meeting. There are just women of different ages and races. Their prayer becomes more and more animated – black spiritual-like, they sing with swaying hips and eyes looking to the sky. The girl joins the others, but the voice says she is disappointed; this is not the place to seek consolation.

Once again, she is separated from her friend by her inner experiences – and this time, they do not meet at all. He is completely baffled, "why did she just leave." But she is on a "trip" into the depths of the soul – here, everything is reversed. This is something that characterizes, e.g., the realm of the dead and the collective unconscious. She is still unaware of what is happening; "time has run out."

But the other part of her, the dark girl we have met several times before her unconscious femininity, is at the same time on another trip that reveals the deeper purpose of the journey. She goes to a religious meeting. So, there is a spiritual-religious problem in this. She is worried and seeks out the women's group in the foreign country. The male reporter's voice cannot understand this: "Why does she do that; this is not customary." But it clearly has a function: The girl seeks out the primal female orgiastic community in a kind of obsessive ecstasy, hoping to find "consolation" – a word for comfort that has clear religious overtones. Again, music plays a role, this time in the form of song.

As a result of our polarised patriarchal-matriarchal society, the feminine spirit has been left in a primitive state. Our religious concepts lack an expression of female values – and of the feminine form of ecstasy. It is then relegated to the hinterland of the psyche, and much female anger against men is justified by his lack of understanding of the religious-spiritual element in eroticism. However, I believe that it is primarily the woman's task to give the man this understanding, which means that she must win it for herself in order to be able to communicate it. She must consciously connect with the numinous male in order to build this bridge.

In the dream, the dark girl finds no male element, and this may well be the reason for her disappointment – here, she does not find what she is looking for:

> *I look out of the window and see what I recognize as a UFO. I can hardly believe my eyes and call out to my brother: "Come and have a look." Then it comes in; it's something else than we thought. We sit on the floor with it between us; we have to do something with it. My father appears in the open doorway; we exchange a few remarks, and then he leaves again. He's naked, and so are we; it occurs to me that he has a woman's body, breasts at least.*

What appears to be a UFO but is not must be understood as a symbol of the Self, the unifying symbol between opposites. The dreamer and the brother then represent the male-female pair. And then the father appears in a double-gendered figure. He, too, must be a personification of the archetype of the Self, as the union of male and female, the transpersonal paternal "Ouroboros," whose intrusion into the psyche of the little girl we have already mentioned. Here, however, it occurs in the process of individuation as a vision of the union of the sexes – with numinous overtones. But since it is the father, and not a superior figure, who expresses this union, we must regard it as a preliminary stage. Some of the personal issues are still linked to the father or the father imago.

Part of the fear of the male will naturally be linked to the fear of incest if these problems have not developed naturally. It is very common for fathers to find it quite difficult to deal with the little girl's seductive behavior at the age of 3-4 years because their own feelings of eroticism are not sufficiently differentiated from their sexual feelings. This can easily lead to the father rejecting the little girl's advances too brutally because he unconsciously fears his own instinctive side. In this way, he will convey to the girl the impression that masculinity is "dangerous" if it is accompanied by sexuality. The mother only too willingly supports this perception by her fear of the male. The spiritual and the sexual enter into an unconscious connection, where the spiritual is perceived as positive and the sexual as negative. This blocks the way to the particularly female spirit, where this connection is very necessary. Again, the unconscious carries the process forward:

> I'm with a man; we're also out at sea in a boat. There's always a slightly dangerous atmosphere. Something about a small child that we have almost run over or that has almost drowned. The man has taken it with him for "impure" reasons; he is not a good man. Someone warns him that the Norn "Phrygia" in the sea will take revenge, but he does not believe it. But the sea becomes extremely rough. An arm and hand, a female of enormous size, suddenly appears and pulls him down. The boat, the child, and I are unharmed.

Here, we meet the "impure" man who is a threat to the dreamer – and to the new individuality that is still in the shape of a child. The Norn "Phrygia," the dreamer, is associated with "fear" [frygt in Danish], but curiously enough, in ancient Phoenicia, it is a name for the great goddess. There is no doubt that it is the Great Mother we have in mind here, a life-sized female hand that destroys something dangerously male, leaving the female element unharmed. A Norn is a goddess of fate, and the manifestations of the unconscious, for good or ill, are often characterized by fate. For many events in a person's life, we have no better word; they are greater and more powerful than our own will. The matriarchal psyche bows to fate and lives in accordance with it, hence the traditional association of women with the art of fortune-telling, premonitions, and trance states. Patriarchal consciousness struggles against fate, and sometimes the 'hero' also overcomes it. The male individuation process has a more 'heroic' character of tasks, challenges, defeated enemies, and won battles. Female individuation consists more of bringing oneself into line with one's inner values, an attunement, a surrender to the conditions of the journey, an exchange of love with the various elements encountered, and a ritual attitude.

Phase IV, The Lover of the Green World

> Dream: *Together with a man, I have reached a small chapel. I think I decorated it myself. You kneel on the floor, on stalls marked with a pattern, like two ovals crossing each other. The floor plan itself is almost shaped like a four-leaf clover. There is no furniture and no roof, but a kind of statue of gods in niches, at least in the small sanctuary where I am sitting. (Almost in the stem of the four-leaf clover.) While I am sitting and praying, the full moon comes out – I call the man, for him to look, too – it has very clearly a man's face.*

There is no doubt that the dreamer has arrived at a better place than "the female religious community." Here, she has her animus with her, and she has organized the place herself, i.e., the foundation is her own individual standpoint. The four-leaf clover shape and the two intersecting ovals are images of wholeness. At the same time, the chapel is connected to nature itself since there is no roof. This is reminiscent of the old Nordic "shrines," which were also out in nature, placed in especially sacred places. And then the moon appears, in all its full splendor, with a man's face.

That the moon appeared with a man's face was a great surprise to the dreamer, who had always associated the moon with something feminine. From the point of view of the history of religion, however, this is not a great surprise; although the moon is very often associated with the feminine, the moon god or moon spirit, being the source of all fertility, is perceived as the 'lord of women,' the fertilizer. Mircea Eliade devotes a chapter in 'Patterns in Comparative Religion' to the moon and its mysticism. He summarises the 'lunar themes' as a. fertility (water, vegetation, women, mythological ancestor) b. periodic regeneration (snake symbolism, death and rebirth at initiations, etc.) c. time and destiny (the moon 'measures' or weaves destiny and connects various cosmic layers and homogeneous realities) d. transformation (light-darkness, full moon-new moon, the upper world, and the underworld, enemy brothers, good and evil) and the balance between the existent and the non-existent, the latent and the actualized.

The dominant idea of all, says Eliade, is rhythm. Everything changes and becomes something else. No transformation is final but is part of a cyclical pattern.

Erich Neumann, in 'The Moon and Matriarchal Consciousness,' explains the connection between the moon and matriarchal consciousness. He says that here, the Self dominates as the male moon, contained in a greater totality in which the whole dark and mysterious process of growth takes place. This totality is the Great Mother, the totality of the nocturnal. By experiencing this ancient wholeness, the dreamer is brought into contact with the root of all growing things, not projected into the world as something coming from gods or spirits but by a close connection with the creative activity of the unconscious. The opposite, negative side of the Moon archetype shows itself in the unconscious obsession with consciousness, wild, uncontrolled ecstasy, violent mood swings, and/or spiritual obsession with "magical" powers.

We have already seen how the dreamer basically feared this but has now contacted the rhythmic potential in a positive way. Women have an instinctive biological relationship to the lunar rhythms through their own rhythms, menstruation, and pregnancy. These rhythms, of course, again have a special relationship with music and ecstasy through music, as we have already seen in several dreams. But in this dream, it is the contemplative side of the activity of the moon spirit that predominates.

In a way, one could say that the dreamer has now completed the task she was given in the underground dwelling of the elves– she has purified the matriarchal psyche's own inherent image of the male, and it has been returned to its original numinous position as moon spirit. This opens the possibility of a male structuring activity in the female psyche on the female's own terms. This is revealed in a dream two nights later:

> *Suddenly, I had to sit an exam that I had forgotten about. My teacher enters the room – he smiles happily at me because he thinks I'm a good student. However, I have almost nothing to say. Later, I keep escaping down into caves and back up again. Finally, down in the caves, the guy I was running with disappears; I'm on my own. I get deep into the ground and into some very large caves – full of people. There goes a young blond man; he is very dirty and has a strange way of moving like all the cave dwellers. But he is nice; I talk to him. He hasn't seen the light for many years. His father had a mine that they put all their efforts into, and the mine collapsed, and they had to live in the underground. – I think the father had to flee; there were some workers who were buried by the mine collapse. – Food is scarce in the underworld. By the way, today is his birthday. I think he's nice, so I give him a kiss on the cheek and say happy birthday, which confuses him a bit because no one has ever done that before.*

The forgotten exam and the next phase of the dream have the deepest connection with each other. On her journey into matriarchal consciousness, the dreamer forgets her skills in the patriarchal world. The teacher considers her a good student, but she has nothing to say in response. Being a good student is typical for the girl in male society. Kirsten Larsen and Harriet Bjerrum Nielsen have written about 'Girls in the Classroom.' It is clear from their research that boys and girls behave in completely different ways at school and have different interests. "Whereas the boys try to redefine the classroom conversation on a relational level into an equal conversation – the dream of dialogue pedagogy – the girls themselves maintain an asymmetrical teacher-student relationship. The boys' comments can often be too many. But the girls constantly remind the teacher of the basic authoritarian structure of teaching, and this is uncomfortable, not least for the progressive teacher. Therefore, the girls are actually a bit annoying in their politeness!

On the other hand, the girls' politeness and passivity are conditions for the realization of the lesson. Therefore, the teacher still has to reinforce it positively by praising it." By observing the children's behavior and listening to their conversations outside the classroom, the two researchers concluded about why boys and girls behave so differently. "The boys' behavior can be interpreted as an expression of a power strategy. The boys seek power in relation to the boy hierarchy; the girls seek intimacy and affirmation in relation to a partner – either the teacher or a friend. If this interpretation is correct, then we have a key to understanding girls' adaptation to the student role."

However, this does not necessarily mean that girls are more authoritarian than boys: "Authority is accepted, but it does not interest her. The acceptance of Authority has become the condition of love, and girls have apparently learned to accept the price of love. In this way, obedience in girls and obedience in boys are probably two different things." We can see, then, that what goes on deep in the unconscious of an adult woman has a direct link to everyday life. This is a collective problem, and its transcendence is a milestone in the psychological development of an adult woman in order to become an individual personality in her own right. In a patriarchal society, what we here call the matriarchal consciousness is reduced to politeness and getting on with each other on a friendship level. Consequently, through the influence of society, the woman cannot develop her Eros consciousness into something more comprehensive or culture-creating until she has differentiated her female side and 'liberated' that part of the animus that is associated with the Great Mother.

The price our dreamer pays is that she stops being a good student and must stop measuring her performance in the eyes of the teacher. And then she can meet the buried lunar animus, the one who was buried deep in the cave systems, in the womb of the Great Mother after the mine collapse. Today is his birthday! Nor is this a coincidence; in a certain sense, he is born precisely because of the dream self's contact with him.

Phase V: The Shadow

The Moon spirit also has its dark time, an expression of danger and evil. During this time, the demonic forces of the unconscious prevail, and the negative tendency of the Great Mother to devour her own children comes to the fore. In this context, this means that the elements of consciousness as 'children' of the unconscious are in danger of slipping away again. We see this in a dream a few months later:

> Several times in the streets, I have noticed a man who is always looking at me. Something about him makes me uneasy. He is a good-looking man, dark with a greyish tinge to his hair, about 30 years old, wearing a black leather jacket and black striped trousers. Then I'm at a party, I think, in a garden. A man makes a pass at me; he's a bit fat, and I don't want anything to do with him. I said to him: "I don't like you." "You don't?" he says; there's something threatening about him, so I get nervous and start explaining that it's not him I have a problem with, but the fact that he's making a pass at me. – Outside, I see "him" (the dark man) again. Now, he is apparently in the company of 5-6 young men sitting in an open Land Rover that drives quietly past and stops. I am afraid of them. Then we are about to leave the party. It's evening. We are traveling by bus. Eventually only my mum and an old, somewhat frail lady are left, we have got off the bus and have to walk some distance to change to another one. We walk in some rather dark streets, it's sleet and a bit slippery, and I support the

old lady's arm as I desperately look around for a taxi, but none shows up. In the distance, I see the Land Rover approaching. I let go of the old lady and ran to the nearest staircase, where there was a light on the ground floor. I ring the doorbell. A young man answers. "Can I please use your phone to call a car – there are some men after me." He measures me and slowly begins to give me his opinion on how it happened. I get the impression that he thinks I'm probably to blame. I'm terrified. "But I'm so scared," I say. It's urgent, I think, because "he" has now taken up position outside in the dim light of a street lamp. He has what looks like a bandage around one leg and foot, and leaning on a stick, he stares straight at me. The bandage is a kind of camouflage. But the otherwise nice young man smiles slightly at my anxiety. "Well, that's good," he says (as if he thinks I'm now realising the consequences of what I've got myself into). I don't realize whether he hasn't realized the gravity of the situation, or doesn't care, or something else. But now I am alone on the landing, which is open, with only latticework between "him" and me. "He" is approaching. I see, to my horror, that he has an injection needle in his hand, with which he lashes out at my thigh. – I just manage to pull my leg back, and then I wake up.

It is a perilous situation right from the start, with the "demonic" dark man already looking out for the dreamer. But in daylight, at the party, she is apparently relatively safe, even though a certain fear of the male is already expressed in her encounter with the "little fat" man. It is almost as if her very fear of him brings the dark man closer; just then, the Land Rover pulls up. Then they head home; it is dark and sleet, a fitting expression for the "climate of the soul." There is danger in the air, and, as expected, the Land Rover reappears. The dreamer then runs away from her mother and the old lady. This is significant: She obviously does not trust her positive relationship with the maternal – and perhaps rightly so, since the old woman is so fragile that she needs to be supported.

In previous dreams, we have already seen how her connection with the matriarchal consciousness was initially weak and how it was strengthened through the positive aspects of the Great Mother. But we also saw in the dream, where she danced in and out of the caves with the men – but would not sleep with any of them, that there was a deep and partly unconscious fear of the orgiastic surrender. When her friend reproached her for her provocative movements, she denied them with the rational explanation that there was music and that she was watching her behavior. In this dream, rational explanations no longer work: She is afraid of the demonic man from beginning to end, without realizing what he wants from her. Once again, she escapes into a rational, patriarchal attitude by turning to the "nice" young man. But he does not react at all as expected. He seems to enjoy the fact that she has been put in this situation, and probably rightly so. Through her anxiety, she is forced to experience the conflict with the dark animus figure.

He is a dangerous figure – but he springs from the matriarchal psyche, not the patriarchal. He represents the dark side of the lunar spirit and the danger of possession of consciousness. His intention is to inject her with something – obviously with the intention of depriving her of will and consciousness. This is what she fears most of all.

At the same time, there is an underlying sexual symbolism: His bandaging of the leg and foot makes the leg appear swollen. We are reminded of Oedipus, whose name means "Swollen-Foot." In Freudian psychology, he represents the incestuous longing for the mother. It could also be said that he represents a stage of the male psyche still under the domination of the Great Mother, whose phallic power is bound to her. The injection needle, too, of course, has the character of a phallic intrusion; there is an underlying rape motif. The dreamer had two associations with this rape motif. One was a childhood memory that came to mind. When she was 7-8 years old, she and another little friend had been attacked by some slightly older boys. One of them had said something about not being able to get her trousers off, the way she was kicking. Her friend had already run away, and she managed to free herself and run away without consciously recognizing it as anything other than an ordinary fight.

The second association went to a film about a dark man pursuing a young woman. In the film, he was waiting for her everywhere. When they finally make contact, she thinks he must be deeply in love with her. They go on a picnic, and in the forest, they sink into the grass. The girl thinks this is the beginning of sexual intercourse. But the man kills her.

Again, we are led to an archetypal pattern: the deathly marriage. Again, we find a parallel in the Demeter myth, where Hades brutally robs Kore and abducts her to the underworld. In the Demeter myth, Demeter herself is gone and cannot prevent the event, but even Mother Earth seems to agree, for she is actually the one who sets the trap for the girl. "Gaia has now kindly let a narcissus sprout for the girl to fool," the myth says. Furthermore, it is said that no one heard the girl's screams "but from her cave, Perasios' daughter heard it with pain, Hékate, she who is proud of her splendor and the shining linen veil." Hékate is the moon goddess, and the fact that she hears it from her cave must simply mean that it takes place while the moon is not visible in the sky. During the dark time, demonic forces threaten.

But we get another important piece of information: The dark man's bandage is "camouflage"; something here is not what it seems, and the dream does not lead to any solution to the problem. There seems to be an insufficient differentiation of male and female elements in the psyche. A new dream takes us even deeper into the unconscious:

Something has happened on the ground – a flood or something. – It's still raining, and everything is very wet. But I don't see any dead people. I am in a foreign place, a sort of school, I think. Now, we all have to leave for our real home. I also talked to my father and mother, who are nearby. Dad says that his home is somewhere else and that he has to be separated from Mum. Mum takes it very calmly, but I get a bit angry. He could have waited to tell me when they were going to be traveling together most of the way anyway. I met a girl I knew; we talked about the long journeys we had made, and suddenly, I remember that as a child, I flew around the moon in a rocket with Mum and Dad. I clearly remember the feeling of the vast space around me and the sight of the moon very close by.

There is also something about a very young man, very handsome, who loves me. I think we have a short relationship, but then he has to leave to become a man. Everything is kind of chaotic, without rules. At one point I have to go into a town to get supplies. A young man is going with me; I'm waiting for him, he's annoyingly slow. Eventually, he comes. I am holding a large, flat basket containing, among other things, a pineapple. "Look," I say suddenly, "a tree has come into the leaf within the basket." The palm leaves on the pineapple form a circle; they radiate out like spokes in a wheel.

We are cycling downtown. In a shop, I see a lot of people; I say something to my companion that I don't understand why they have tied themselves to it when they could be free. One of them is X; she is rushing around in a hurry. – In another shop we enter, a lady comes in and shows some red clogs she has just bought – she praises them highly. Since I actually need some good shoes for the journey ahead, I take a closer look at them, and they are really something special. There are narrow gold moldings on the heel to strengthen them, but they are narrower and lighter than clogs usually are, and the sole is made of a cork-like material. The lady says she didn't think they were available anymore, but you can get them in the shop down the street (the shop I saw X in).

A deluge is at once a wiping out of old ills and a new beginning. Here, the emphasis is on the new beginning – everyone has to go to their "real" home, i.e., the elements of the psyche have to be placed in the right way, as they were meant to be from the beginning. That is why the parents must be separated. It is an important motif. In terms of developmental history, it belongs to early childhood, when the intrusion of the male ouroboros was supposed to lead to a separation of the male and the female. Archetypically, it is a separation of the world's parents. In many mythologies, the first act of the main god is to separate heaven and earth, which until then had been in close embrace and incessantly producing offspring. This act makes the world habitable for humans so that an ordered society can emerge. As this is a woman's dream, it also involves a temporary identification with the Great Mother – hence the motif of the beautiful youth who must pass away to become a man. This corresponds to the Great Mother's son-lovers, who are usually beautiful young men – Adonis, for example. But in the mother-son-lover relationship, the son is never allowed to pass away to become a man – he inevitably dies in the myths. Admittedly, his rebirth is included, but it is an eternal, closed cycle in which the son represents the principle of growth, vegetation, and crops. The Great Mother has no equal partner at that stage of development.

In the dream, we are taken back to an even earlier motif – a recollection of the dream of the time when father, mother, and child circled the moon. This refers to a completely undifferentiated primordial state of consciousness, an ouroboros state, in which neither father nor mother has separated from the element of consciousness (the rocket). It corresponds to the infant's total dependence on the mother, with its rudimentary consciousness system circling in a fixed orbit around the mother self.

Another unifying symbol is found in the pineapple, which suddenly opens with radiating leaves just as her companion appears. They are going into town for provisions. This motif is not surprising because, as we have seen, the dreamer still does not have enough anchorage in her female consciousness – she needs extra sustenance for the journey ahead.

And it's not just about food. The dreamer also needs a good pair of shoes for the journey ahead. Shoes are linked to female identity. Shoes are what we stand on, our foundation. But at the same time, they also have a female sexual character because of their shape. These shoes are sold in a shop where she sees X. This X is a very practical friend, sweet and warm, but also, in the dreamer's opinion, too dependent on convention. So, she is a shadow figure, representing the opposite of the dreamer's opinion that these shop assistants could be free and not tied to their business. However, this business turns out to be more valuable than the dreamer realized because it is the only place to get such shoes.

The motif points to a weak point in the dreamer: The adaptation to reality and the environment. The shoes compensate for a tendency to lose grounding and perhaps also emotional contact with her surroundings. The shoes give her a more solid foothold in a female' space.' The preciousness is emphasized by the gold strips. The Gold stands for a spiritual element.

The spiritual-religious issue is not forgotten; it is directly addressed in a subsequent dream:

I'm in a church room. There are some deep corridors underneath that we descend into. Some say it smells (associated with sewage systems). But it doesn't bother me – I want to move on.

Church space represents our habitual concepts of a sacred place where the spirit and God are present. The ordinary Christian mind has no concept of the deep corridors that lie beneath. But our form of religion, of course, stands on the shoulders of other and older religious forms, which have then been largely "abolished." This means that they have sunk into the collective unconscious. Here, we are concerned first and foremost with the subterranean elements. As we have seen, these are linked to the creative power of nature, as well as to sexuality and the life of instinct in general. They contain all the elements that the "father religion," with its "high" spiritual values, could not accept. But for a woman, it is, of course, inevitable – if she is to find herself also in a spiritual sense – that she encounters these collectively repressed contents. For the female spirit is buried deep in the womb of the earth, and it is of great importance to bring it out. We shall see what the outcome of this journey is:

Standing with someone and looking out over some excavations, I am
shown the past in the form of one church remains, well, altar, and
stonework after another. They are right next to each other on a sloping
terrain but staggered in time back to primitive societies. I remark to the
man I'm with that they – our ancestors – don't seem to have needed
much space (the foundations show that the buildings were quite
small). He replies that for them, "space" was not as important as
"level". (Already in the dream, it is clear that this is a play on words,
two words for the room, where "space" is the simple spatial extent,
while "level" implies a psychic/spiritual level).

This dream demonstrates some features of the functioning of
the feminine spirit. Neumann (The Moon and the Matriarchal
Consciousness) states: "Matriarchal wisdom is paradoxical. It never
separates or juxtaposes opposites with the clear discrimination of
patriarchal consciousness; rather, it relates them to one another by
an "as well as" or an "also." From this point of view – not to be
misinterpreted – matriarchal consciousness is relativistic, for it is
less orientated to the absolute unambiguity of truth than to wisdom
which remains embedded in a cosmo-psychological system of
ever-changing forces". (p. 57) Thus, we see in this dream that the
different religious remains of the ancestors are perceived as
coherent; there is, e.g., no Christian-pagan opposition. All these
ruins are a manifestation of the sacred. There is a good reason for the
curious play on words that occurs in the dream.

The patriarchal ego-orientated consciousness is "space"
orientated; it wants to conquer as much space as possible; also,
culturally, it has been – and is – imperialistic. It has also endeavored
to free itself from its unconscious presuppositions and strives to rely
solely on its own will. It is self-sufficient, which the matriarchal
consciousness never is.

It is a man who shows the dreamer these excavations. It is
the animus in its positive function as a guide in the inner universe.
But he is not the ruler of it. In the dream with the full moon with the

man's face, we saw the moon as a male manifestation of the center of the inner world, but the moon also has – of course – a feminine manifestation of the highest form of the female spirit, the figure of Sophia (= wisdom).

Phase VI. The final descent to the nadir

Dream: *Something about traveling. Mum wakes me up very early. I think we live on a rocky island. I'm going somewhere; something is going on underground, maybe some kind of female' initiation ceremony.' There's horror involved and dark secrets. – My task is to somehow shine a light on it, which is difficult because I have to go through it and keep an overview at the same time.*

Here the mother has taken the lead and leads the dreamer into the female initiation ceremony in the underground realms. It seems to be a dark and obscure place, and the paradoxical difficulty for the woman is emphasized: She must simultaneously experience this and yet see it with her consciousness. Immediately afterward comes the following dream:

As a birthday present from my grandmother, I get a bottle of fine old red wine worth DKK 600. She has thought carefully about what she could give me that I would not refuse.

It is a very old custom that an initiation is considered a new birth. In many societies, it was customary that when a young person was initiated as an adult, they were also given a new name. Here, at least, there is a birthday present from the grandmother. So, the mother archetype is now entirely positively constellated. The grandmother's gift, we are told, has been carefully considered – something the dreamer would not reject. So, we can probably allow ourselves to see it symbolically. Wine is often – even in the Christian communion – seen as an image of the spirit. "Spiritus" is both alcohol and spirit. The intoxication, the exhilaration that wine can bring, is related to spiritual ecstasy. Thus, in the Dionysian mysteries, which, as mentioned earlier, attracted women in particular. The value of this gift is specifically indicated: DKK 600.

The number six is a 'perfect' number in the sense that the numbers that add up to it (1, 2, 3) also add up to six (1x2x3=6, 1+2+3=6). Often, six is perceived as a doubling of three. Marie Louise von Franz writes in "Number and Time" p. 109f: "Threefold rhythms are most probably connected with processes in space and time or with their realization in consciousness. In physics also, one of the most important groups is that of rotations in six dimensions". The Chinese I Ching, the book of transformations, uses 64 hexagrams (six-line figures) to express how cosmic transformations are changed in time and space and in relation to the human' user' of the hexagrams. These six-line figures are to be understood as combinations of eight different trigrams.

In the Tantric chakra system, six is depicted as a six-pointed star in the Anahata chakra, the heart center. Again, it is formed by two triangles, one facing up and one facing down, which in themselves symbolize the union of the male and female principles. In Tantric philosophy, the union of these two principles is an expression of the sexual union between man and woman and also of the divine cosmic creative power. It is through this sexual-spiritual dynamic that the world comes into being all, and man's return to cosmic unity is also expressed in sexual symbolics. Strangely enough – from our habitual thinking – in this philosophy it is the female principle, Shakti, that is the active creator. The universe, as it manifests itself, is mastered by the female spirit. Both the 'gross' matter and the 'finer' matter that we are accustomed to attribute to the activity of the mind.

We could, therefore, assume from this dream that the unconscious is preparing for the unification of opposites and their integration into consciousness. This turned out to take time and pass through a major crisis. This type of crisis corresponds to a death experience in which everything disintegrates, and all old values lose their meaning. However, when consciousness can bear to participate in it, it becomes more than a typical female depression (where consciousness is unable to keep up with what is happening deep in the unconscious); it becomes the real condition for rebirth. Sylvia Brinton Perera, in her excellent book "Descent to the Goddess. A Way of Initiation for Women has given a general account of the phases of the crisis and its psychological meaning through an interpretation of the Sumerian myth of the descent and return from the realm of death of the sky queen Inanna and the Goddess of death Ereshkigal.

Here, the descent is successful, and we must leap forward to a dream that resumes the cave motif, showing how much has happened in the meantime:

> *In Crete with my boyfriend. I've spoken to my dark friend before, and she told me about the New Year's Eve celebrations in the caves of Crete. You go down into the caves in a group, men and women, and in torchlight, you have a sexual orgy. I ask, a little worried; what if there's a man you don't want to make love to? "Then he couldn't touch you," she says. I'm now quite keen on this party, which I'm attending with my boyfriend. I think there are three other men and ditto women in the group, including myself. At least one of the men is very handsome. There is also one who is fat, and I am thinking that I don't want anything to do with him. But the guide says that rape is strictly forbidden.*

Again, we see the Dionysian motif, the ecstatic orgy. But this time, she is neither unconscious nor afraid, and she has her animus with her. He no longer stands outside and gives rational warnings. Moreover, the old problem of rape seems to have been solved: It is simply no longer possible. This means, of course, that she no longer has to fear the unconscious state of obsession that used to threaten her if she gave in to her orgiastic urges. The differentiation towards the masculine has progressed: There is a fat, unattractive man and a very handsome man, in addition, of course, to her boyfriend. We already encountered the fat man as an expression of the negative masculine in the dream with the demonic, dark man with the syringe, where her rejection of the fat man led her into a confrontation with the more demonic and, therefore, far more dangerous animus. Now, he is no longer dangerous. Now one must ask: What on earth is the purpose of the dreamer's participation in this New Year's orgy? Why does the "great goddess" seem to demand just this? To answer this question, we must go back to the great goddesses of the Middle East and their priestesses, the hierodules, the "sacred prostitutes. "About them, Esther Harding writes in "Woman's Mysteries" p. 132: "These women were bound to the service of the Goddess, their sexuality, their attraction, their love was not to be used for their own gratification or for the ordinary purposes of human life. They could not unite with a husband, for their female nature was destined for a higher purpose – that of bringing the fertilizing power of the Goddess into effective contact with human life."

Ordinary women were married and expected to live in a monogamous marriage, but tradition also required them to make a sacrifice to the Goddess of love. Harding says,

> To symbolize the truth of God as manifest, potent, in the union of man and woman, that is, of masculine and feminine principles, women, at their initiation into the mysteries of the Great Goddess, sacrificed their virginity in the temple by entering into a hieros gamos, or sacred marriage, which was consummated sometimes with the priest, as representative of the phallic power of the god, sometimes with the phallic image itself, and sometimes with any stranger who might be spending the night in the temple precincts. (p.134).

The rite is a way of expressing that the woman's sexuality is the expression of a divine life force. By absorbing this experience – nowadays, on a psychological level – the archetypal and the human are separated, and only then can the woman essentially give herself freely to a human partner, with the emphasis on the personal relationship between them. In the myth of Amor and Psyche, Psyche prepares for a fatal wedding, but in her first relationship with Amor, she experiences an instinctive and completely impersonal sexual intoxication. They then separate, and only after a long evolution do they meet again on a higher, personal level[14].

Behind the fear of surrender, then, is an inadequate differentiation between the personal and the archetypal. The archetypal female desire for the ecstatic encounter with the unknown stranger becomes a mere sexual indulgence. Erica Jong has described it as 'the frictionless fuck'. A host of female sexual fantasies revolve around this.

In a way, there is a similar archetypal image behind the other sex's impulse for casual sex. For the man, it is an impulse to spread his sperm all over the world. If you only fulfill this sexually, the spiritual aspect is lost. The only place where both aspects can exist at the same time is in the psyche. The archetypal motif must, therefore, be experienced as a spiritual reality in its full dimension. If both man and woman can experience it, sexual intercourse can be both earthly and "heavenly" at the same time: They love each other as individual persons, but at the same time, there is a spiritual experience that the other is all men and all women, that they participate in an eternal fusion of male and female.

We meet the dark friend for the fourth time (also as the master swimmer, (p. 103), as the one who cleans up. (p.111), and the dark girl who went to a religious meeting (p.128). However, she was also present in other dreams not reported here, and it had gradually become clear that she acted as a provocateur and initiator of the dreamer's feminine development. But she was enigmatic and fascinating, something that signaled that she still belonged mainly to the sphere of the unconscious. When an unconscious figure becomes conscious, it loses its allure and becomes a function of consciousness. The fascination then falls instead on the archetypal figure behind it. We shall see how this manifests itself in some dreams that followed in quick succession:

---

[14] See Neumann: Cupid and Psyche.

Fleeing from someone, I find myself at my childhood home, on a grassy meadow that was there. Down by the road are two horses, one is mine, it is grey. The other is white with black spots, it's my dark friend's. I look down at myself; I'm wearing some kind of man's clothes, a peasant's coat, and stockings, I think. I see the dark girl running across the field. I think to myself that I cannot ride away dressed as I am. "They" know my horse and will look for a man. But a couple on another horse, they won't look. I run after the girl, she's shy. "Wait for me," I call. Just before I reach her, it's as if a male figure is already running beside her, my male side, I think. But then she waits; we can ride away on her spotted horse. She sits in front of me. I stroke her breast. It's arousing as if it were being done to myself.

The scene of the dream is the childhood home. As I mentioned at the beginning, the personal role model for the dark friend seems to be a little girl from whom she was separated precisely by moving to this home. It seems logical that the union must take place where the separation occurred. Not in the area of the settlement itself, but on the grass meadow, a place that lay undeveloped. A small piece of "wild nature," which is always mythically dominated by the Great Mother. It points to something that has not been repressed because it has never yet been made conscious. That the problem has an instinctive basis is suggested by the fact that both girls have horses. The dreamer's horse is gray. Gray is a mixture of colors, or as the saying goes, "in the dark, all cats are gray" – the colors are not visibly distinguishable from each other, that is, something undifferentiated. The friend's horse is black and white – the two colors you can mix on the palette to get gray. So, it seems that the dreamer is still undifferentiated in terms of her female instinct.

This corresponds to the dreamer being dressed in a man's suit. Her female Self is, therefore, male in color. But it is a medieval-styled clothing, which today could easily pass for females: Short dress with stockings. In fact, it is typical of many modern women that their ego becomes male-coloured. There had also been a number of animus problems for this dreamer, but they had been solved. But apparently, there is still a little more to go before she can "get away" from some pursuers. She must unite with her dark friend and ride away on her horse. For a moment, it seems as if an animus is already running at her side, a small reminiscence of the characteristic shadow-animus marriage. But here, it is no longer an obstacle, presumably because the animus had already been largely integrated. That integration itself could be responsible for the male clothing; there is a preponderance of males in the consciousness that needs to be balanced with something female.

Clothing is something you wear on the outside. As the two ride away together, the dark girl sits in front, as if on the outside, and their relationship borders on identification, for the touching of her breast feels as if it were done to the dreamer himself. With this integration, part of the fascination with the dark friend falls away, and another archetype emerges:

I am in another time; it seems medieval. I'm employed in the Queen's court, along with my dark friend. She is the Queen's personal handmaiden. I am very captivated by the Queen, who is a beautiful golden-haired woman. One morning, I ran with my friend to the Queen's room. At one point, I accidentally knock over a glass of tea, I lie on the floor and wipe it up. I really want the Queen to notice me, and now her friend has finished her work and left, leaving us alone. She is not angry at my clumsiness but sits down in a chair and starts talking to me. I crawl closer and closer and finally put my head on her knee, full of love. There is a kind of sadness in her expression. Is it something to do with the king not being there?

The beautiful, golden-haired Queen can be seen as a personification of the archetype of the Self, as she is an entirely superior female figure. The dark friend is the Queen's personal handmaiden, i.e., her activities have been subordinated to those of the Self. Her activity in the psyche has led the dreamer to an encounter with the female Self, to which the dreamer literally submits. The concluding remark that there is a kind of sadness about the Queen, perhaps because the king is gone, suggests that the masculine part of the Self is not yet united with the feminine part. Of course, the Self as a totality contains both the masculine and the feminine within it.

Phase VII Ascension and Return to the Known World

> Dream: *I am in a place, a kind of community. There is a kind of "stall" where the dark girl is sitting. The opening in the stall shows her as if she were some kind of icon, and she also has a Madonna-like status. Suddenly, she becomes strange, withdraws completely into herself, and shuts herself up in her own room where she doesn't want to be in contact with anyone. I get in there, however, and I embrace her sexually. She has an intense orgasm. This somehow seems to release her; now she tells me that she has a relationship with a bearded man, and now she dares to admit it openly. They are seen together.*

Here, the dark girl has a spiritual status. She acts almost as an object of worship, but only her head and shoulders are visible, as in an icon. This corresponds to the female spiritual ideal of purity that I mentioned earlier and which Jung described as destructive to the female ideal of completeness. We have seen earlier how the dark girl helped to bring the dreamer into contact with the matriarchal roots of the "caves." In that direction, downwards, the problem was not so much chastity or purity as it was "fear of rape. "Now the direction is more "upwards" in the spiritual sphere. The dark woman, not content to be locked up in her exalted position as a virgin spirit, rebels and becomes completely inaccessible.

Once again, the solution appears to be instinctive – the dreamer has intercourse with her, and she has an orgasm. In this breach of chastity, she dares to admit that she has a relationship with "a bearded man." She wants to express this relationship with the male freely. It is as if the dreamer herself has focussed too much on spiritual development. The dark girl also wants an expression that is more instinctive. We met the bearded man as a relief in the underground dwelling of the elf girls, and we have seen how the development of the spiritual side of this motif became the male moon. Obviously, it should not be forgotten that the bearded man as Kabir stands for the breeding principle. Only his head was shown in relief, just as the dark girl in the dream is seen as a 'breast image.' In fact, the dreamer became pregnant. Conception must have been around this time, but it was by no means planned. However, she had no major problems accepting it as a fact. But if anyone were to infer from this that I generally consider the pinnacle of female development to be pregnancy and motherhood, then she had better read the book again!

For this woman, her pregnancy signaled that she had succeeded in integrating that part of her femininity that is linked to the instinctive, biological basis. She no longer feared that having a child and the attachments it would entail would rob her of opportunities for more spiritually-centered activities. Precisely because she had arrived at a secure experience of who she was, she could confidently embark on the next phase of transformation. Namely, that which pregnancy and motherhood can represent for the woman if she is spiritually capable of co-experiencing it. But that is another story. It is also a very old story since this form of creation was the only acceptable or possible one for women in the past. This is no longer the case, as the steadily declining birth rate testifies. Even those women who, for a number of years, find the biological side of womanhood fully satisfactory are sooner or later confronted with the question of the growth of their own personality. This, therefore, is what I have concentrated on.

I have tried to show how deeply you have to delve into the symbolic world of the unconscious in order, as a woman, to come to terms with conflicts that are not just personal but cultural destiny. Or, to put it another way, I do not think that we, as women, can really change culture without having personally experienced its deepest preconditions and integrated this material into our consciousness.

The result will not be a superwoman. It will be a woman who is what she is. Some people might ask, well, is that really all there is to it? Was it just what came out of all those big pictures? I do not think it is "just." To become what you are, and at the same time to be in living connection with the creative well of all consciousness, is quite a lot. In such a question, there is an urge for a final answer, a final solution to it all. If you feel that way, you have to go to the absolute solution of a religious system. To me, part of the answer lies in stopping asking the question in that way. The final answer to life, as we know it, is death. Life itself consists of an infinite series of transformations that must be experienced. The impulses for them come to us as destiny, both from without and from within. Each new phase of life makes new demands, and any inability to fulfill them, i.e., to transform, gives rise to neurotic patterns.

How much more difficult is it to cope with these transformations at a time when culture itself is changing? The opportunity to contact those deep layers of the unconscious, where the transformation is reflected and to further integrate these images into consciousness, is not available to everyone. For many, the cost will still be too high – and I am not referring here to a possible analysis fee! Adapting to one's true nature as a woman can still mean becoming so maladjusted to one's surroundings that it takes more than ordinary strength to go through with it.

Those women who are not yet capable of such self-realization may, however, find some comfort in the thought that their problems are not only due to their own shortcomings and the heavy burdens of the past – but also that deep in their souls, they are suffering from the labors of an as yet unborn future

Bibliography

- Atwood Margaret. *Up to the Surface*. Copenhagen, Denmark: Lindhardt og Ringhof, 1983.
- Dowling Colette. *The Cinderella Complex*. Copenhagen: Lindhardt og Ringhof, 1981.
- Eliade Mircea. *Patterns in Comparative Religion*. London: Sheed and Ward, 1958.
- Eliade Mircea. *The History of Religious Ideas*. Copenhagen: Gyldendal 1983.
- Franz Marie Louise von. *Number and Time*. Evanston: Northwestern University Press, 1974.
- Franz Marie Louise von. *An Interpretation of Apuleius' Golden Ass*. Dallas: Spring Publications, 1980.
- Franz Marie Louise von. *Interpretation of Fairytales*. Dallas: Spring Publications, 1982.
- Goethe Johann Wolfgang von. *Faust*. Translated by P. Hansen. Copenhagen, Denmark: Gyldendal, 1902.
- Harding M. Esther. *Woman's Mysteries*. New York: Harper Colophon Books, 1976.
- Homer. *Hymns*. Translated by Alex Garff and Leo Hjortsø. Copenhagen: Gyldendal, 1961.
- Jacobi Jolande. C.G. The psychology of Jung. Copenhagen: Gyldendals Uglebøger, 1976.
- Jacobi Jolande. *The Way of Individuation*. New York: Meridian, 1983.
- Jensen Karsten Sejr. *Witchcraft in Denmark*. 1500-1588. Thesis at the University of Copenhagen. Copenhagen 1980.
- Jung C.G. Collected Works (GW). Zurich: Rascher, 1958-1970. Olten: 1971-
- Jung C.G. and Kerényi Karl. *Introduction to a Science of Mythology*. London: Routledge & Kegan Paul, 1951 (see also: GW9,1,1976).
- Jung C.G. *Answers to Job's questions*. Copenhagen: Gyldendal, 1973 (see also: GW 11, 1963). Jung C.G. Die Frau in Europa. GW 10, 1974.
- Jung C.G. *Psychological typology*. Copenhagen: Gyldendals Uglebøger, 1975 (see also: GW 6,1960).
- Jung C.G. *Memories, dreams and thoughts*. Copenhagen, Denmark: Lindhardt og Ringhof, 1984.
- Jung Emma. *Animus and Anima*. Zurich: Spring Publications, 1978.
- Kerényi Karl. Hermes. *Guide of Souls*. Zurich: Spring Publications, 1976.
- Larsen Kirsten and Nielsen Harriet Bjerrum. *Girls in the Classroom Public*. In: Pigeopdragelse/Pigeliv. Copenhagen: Emmeline, 1982.

- Nichols Sallie. *Jung and Tarot. An Archetypal Journey.* New York: Samuel Weiser, 1980.
- Neumann Erich. *Zur Psychologie des Weiblichen* (Umkreisung der Mitte, Vol. II) Zurich, 1953.
- Neumann Erich. *The Great Mother.* New York: Princeton University Press, 1963.
- Neumann Erich. *Amor and Psyche.* Copenhagen: Niels Bing Publishers, 1965.
- Neumann Erich. *The Moon and Matriarchal Consciousness.* In: "Fathers and Mothers". Zurich: Spring Publications, 1973.
- Neumann Erich. *The Child.* New York/London: Harper Colophon Books, 1976.
- Nyborg Eigil. *The Inner Line in Hans Christian Andersen's fairy tales. Andersen's Fairy Tales.* Copenhagen, Denmark: Gyldendal, 1983.
- Perera Sylvia Brinton. *Descent to the Goddess. A Way of Initiation for Women.* Toronto: Inner City Books, 1981.
- Pratt, Annis. *Surfacing and the Rebirth Journey.* In: "The Art of Margaret Atwood". Ed. Davidson A.E. and C.N. Toronto, 1981.
- Teglbjærg Åse Stubbe: *Live your Dreams.* Klitrose, 1984.
- Wheelwright Joseph B. *Saint George and the Dandelion.* C.G. Jung Institute of San Francisco, 1982.
- Wolff Toni. *Studies on C.G. Jung's Psychology.* Zurich: Daimons Verlag, 1981.

Made in the USA
Las Vegas, NV
21 November 2024

12276074R00104